bullet bob world

Wisdom of an 85 year old dog

Spirituality, Religion and Politics

A guide to self realization

Clues to higher understanding

Proposed reform for world governments and religions

Proposed reform for USA

THIS IS A MUST READ
FOR EVERYONE

bullet bob

Why bullet bob a dog?   Everyone loves and trusts pets, and pets get attention!

Who is bullet bob?

bullet bob is Robert Emmet Kemper. Born March 11, 1931 in Saint Louis Missouri where he attended and graduated from Lindenwood Grade School and Southwest High School. He played marbles and flipped war cards for keeps, played softball, baseball, basketball and never missed a day of school. He sold St Louis Morning Globe News for three years which afforded expert at penny pinball machines.

In 1949 he began a college career which included attendance at S.E. Missouri State, U of Missouri, Washington U in Saint Louis, U of Texas Arlington, and at age of 56, San Diego Golf Academy. He received a BS Degree in Math and Physical Science from University College Washington U, St Louis in 1958. He received a two-year Certificate in Golf Facility Management at the golf academy where he earned Players Credential, Club Repair Certification and graduated Valedictorian in 1988. He accumulated sufficient college credit for majors in Business Administration and Accounting.

In 1953 he was drafted into the US Army where he completed basic training at Fort Riley, KA and completed intelligence analyst training at the Army Counter Intelligence Corps (CIC) facility in Baltimore, MD. He served with the 115th CIC Detachment in San Francisco, CA. Upon discharge in 1955 returned to St Louis.

His work profession began as a Chemist and Production Supervisor at Modern Dental Materials while attending night school at Washington U. Upon graduation he was offered a job as Planning Engineer at McDonnell Aircraft and spent nine years working on major aerospace projects including Mercury Spacecraft, F4 Fighter, Apollo Spacecraft, TFX Fighter Escape System attaining status of Senior Plant-wide Planner. Also, he served as planner for advanced aircraft design and study activity at McDonnell. In 1967 he moved to Denver, CO to take a position of Assistant Chief Engineer and later Test Director at Stanley Aviation. He worked directly with Bob Stanley who was one of America's aviation heroes. Late 1968 he moved to Dallas, TX to take charge of Ling Tempco Vought Aerospace design department cost and schedule functions; a workforce of 1600 engineers working multi projects. Mid 1972 he returned to Denver, CO to work new business proposals at Martin Marietta Aerospace. One new business proposal was management of a rail transportation system proposal to the US Department of Transportation for the Denver Regional Transportation Department (RTD). RTD invited him along with a group of 12 from Martin Marietta to form the Development Department responsible for proposal preparation. His title was Project Coordinator. Jerry Ford rejected the proposal and sent the funds to Florida in hopes to win the 1976 Presidential Election. However, the Department of Transportation did provide funds to expand the bus system, and he was invited to serve as Manager of Bus Operational Services. In 1980 he returned to Martin Marietta to work new business proposals as Project Planner for Space Shuttle era projects including the LST (Hubble Space Telescope) and Venus Mapper (Magellan). With the infusion of retired pentagon and military into the aerospace industry it has lost innovation and spirit of urgency. Now a breeding ground of costly super welfare and wasteland. In 1987 he took early retirement to peruse the world of golf.

After graduation from the golf academy in 1988 he worked part-tine in the golf shop, did club repair, participated in golf clinics and played on Golden State Golf Tour where he won five senior amateur events. In 1996 he left the country club job in Rancho Santa Fe, CA. He, then participated in the golf club business as buyer, producer and seller of clubs. He attended golf expositions in Orlando and Las Vegas. He was one of the first golf club sellers on Ebay. In 2002 he left the golf business. Never had so much fun!

While working at McDonnell his hobby was bowling. For four years he competed nightly and weekends earning an ABC sanctioned average of 208 over 2200 games. He competed in the St Louis All-Star, St Louis Classic, Champions and Masters Leagues. In 1962-63 season he bowled four ABC sanctioned 300 games which was forth to do that in history. He competed against the professional Budweiser and Falstaff teams. He competed with bowling legends Don Carter, Dick Weber, Ray Bluth, Elvin Mesger and good friend Nelson (Bo) Burton.

While working at RTD he spent weekends in the real-estate business acquiring houses and apartments. He attended class and acquired a real estate sales license. Then, the owner and manager of five rental properties. After 25 years all paid for and 1.3 million dollars equity. Since he has sold three and today lives in one and lease another. In 1972 with the help of two partners acquired two apartment buildings of 49 units in Dallas, TX. Under purchase contract successfully renovated and fully rented the apartments. Later formed a corporation, issued stock and obtained an appraisal netting $200,000 in equity and net worth. Unfortunately, he moved back to Denver and six years later a stock holder acquired majority stock, sold the property, took a management contract and acquired six additional apartment projects for renovation. He was to have 10% of the new business organization. He did not trust and abandoned. Lessons are stay close to your business, and do not trust lawyers.

In 2002 he needed a new adventure, and by happenstance was given a tour of night life in Tijuana(TJ), Mexico by a 16 year old boy. Living in affluent Carmel Del Mar and spending nights and some days in Baja California, he could compare poor and rich society. The affluent seem fearful and live to a beat of the social system drum, however the abominable poor are creative and live to the beat of their individual true center of existence. This was a perfect adventure to study spirituality, world religion and mythology by day and enjoy the dangerous excitement of TJ cultural at night. This was costly and to fund this adventure consisted of collecting rent, gambling at race track and Social Security. Now integrated with the Mexican community, he acquired good friends like dentists, doctors, store owners, bar tenders and prostitutes. Also, he became familiar with the Spanish language. Ah, EE. I, O, OOU, El burro sabe mas que tu! After five years, he was exhausted. Tired but wiser, he sold his townhouse in Carmel Del Mar and moved back to Denver in 2006 to save his real estate investment.

After restructure of finances and real estate he was ready for a new adventure. Again, by happenstance, a Swiss friend who he taught golf, invited him to visit Bangkok, Thailand. From the time he boarded the plane for his first journey to Bangkok till today after spending seven winters in SE Asia, wow, what an exciting experience. Bangkok night life, touring Thailand, Laos, Cambodia and visit Myanmar gives a new perspective to life. Materialism is growing there, but one can feel the beauty of their historical life struggle and the Buddhist spirituality. Saawadee coup. Coup coon coup!

Along the way he married thrice, two daughters, five grandchildren and two great grandchildren. He is much better at divorce than marriage. Well, family is really quite an experience and matters, but sometimes he thinks life is really an individual sport.

Now at home in Lone Tree, Colorado, bullet cleans house, cuts grass, visits Good Will stores, goes to the horse race track in summer, plays golf from the front tees, drives his 1984 Chevy S10 pickup truck and awaits a new adventure. He returns to TJ, Thailand and the golf course, but it ain't the same. He subsidizes a family in Nakhon Sawan, Thailand and pays school tuition for the young lady. He has many great adventure stories to tell, but found no one is interested. Alone in memory he writes **bullet bob world**, and again found little interest. Is bullet bob, the old dog, living the American dream?

bullet bob at Suvarnabhumi International Airport, Bangkok, Thailand 2014

Beat Moor of Zurich, Switzerland and Tikie, at Bridge over River Kwai, Kanchanaburi, Thailand

Chumlong Boonma (Tikie) of Nakhon Sawan, Thai at Kanchanaburi Station 2014

by bullet bob   bullet bob world

CONTENTS

- PREFACE and INTRODUCTION

- BELIEF

- ON BEING

- ABOUT THE HERO

- MEDITATION

- GOD

- ABOUT MORALS AND ETHICS

- CREATION

- RELIGION

- REFORM AND REMEDY (World Religion, World Government, **USA**)

- EPILOG

- JUST A LITTLE MORE

    AGGRIVATION

    ILLUSION

- LOOKING BACK

PREFACE

HOW TO READ bullet bob world

bullet bob dares to present his thoughts on probably the most controversial topics like religion, philosophy and politics.

As you read, please **challenge** every statement, concept, theory, conclusion and interpretation.

When bullet bob tells a story or states his opinion at the end of each topic, let the mind go and turn on the **imagination**. A lot of what bullet bob opines is POETRY.

You will get to know bullet bob, and more importantly, you may be on your way to know yourself. Yes, assist you in the path to self realization.

Does bullet bob have firm belief in **bullet bob world?**   **No**, it is his current state of maturity and consciousness. Is there such a thing as absolute? Is there anything that does not change?

by bullet bob   **bullet bob world**

INTRODUCTION

bullet bob, the old dog, is an alter ego. He thinks he is wisdom. He is very slow by nature, because he often, but not always, thinks before he acts. His wisdom continues to mature, and his thinking seems to change with age as he experiences the world. He continues to expand his knowledge and his understanding with a fairly broad mind, but now he is somewhat perplexed about governmental and religious institution behavior. Both are created by man. Both often corrupted and twisted by man. Survival and ego satisfaction seem to have no boundaries by virtue of mind's ability to justify and rationalize wrong action. Pleasure and greed rule. Therefore, if individual behavior is improved, likewise government and religion are improved. **Fat chance** for this wishful proposition. Never less, bullet bob attempts to present his ideal **prescription to improve mankind by universal emphasis of self realization**. What is your passion? What is your capability? When all of mankind is participating in their passion and government projects and goals are in concert with that passion, we will have a more progressive peaceful earth and transcend individual self-imposed limits. Thus, move rapidly to solve the mysteries of the universe. Again, probably idealistic wishful thinking!

If bullet bob world can help just a few gain a higher level of understanding, he will be gratified, but if he could reach every family and individual on this earth to promote discussion about the matters within this document, that would be the ultimate goal.   For today is seems society tacitly does not permit free speech about political, religious, sex, philosophy and race. It is politically incorrect! In bullet bob's opinion that should change if we as society and the individual are to progress peacefully to our potential. What better place to start this revolution than the family and the schools at all levels. Not recommended at work! Yes, let's have open discussion on these politically incorrect topics without malice and promote a spirit of improving our knowledge about these most important aspects of our society.

bullet bob believes it is not possible for government and religion to eliminate corruption. Well, so far on this earth that has not happened.   bullet bob does not believe that all mankind will shed ignorance and discover passion to fulfill their potential, but we must always aggressively seek to improve government ethics and mankind's understanding and consciousness.

bullet bob senses that materialism is growing throughout the western world. Society focus on money and the things money can buy is growing while focus on religion, especially the morals and ethics, are often ignored. We seem to be living a materialistic mythology where just about everything we participate and speak is assigned a money value. Most of our existence is dedicated to schemes to make money, and often with a "ends justify the means" attitude. Morals and ethics are taking a beating. Most business today is conducted on a very thin line between honesty and dishonesty. Sooner or later society will pay for this questionable moral and ethical behavior. Our governing institutions are in place to maintain trust and fairness, but the money influence from special interest and lobbyist has altered their lawmaking decisions and votes.   Is that corruption or what? Years ago we lived in a predominately spiritual world guided by a mythology of higher principles of morality and ethics, but now materialism seems to rule.

Certainly today we have a much better standard of living, especially in the western world as a result of materialistic mythology, but in my opinion it is bit out of balance because materialistic negative influence on the spiritual and geophysical. The battle is in full force with money and material now winning.

bullet bob makes reference to the "system". General society and governmental law pretty well defined the mythology of how we think, act and speak. Are we **sheeple**? In the western world, after birth we are introduced to religion, attend school, get a job, buy a car, get married, buy a house, raise children, work to retirement, maintain our body, die and receive reward or punishment. Society norms and family have huge influence on the details of these life passages. Most parents do their best to guide and place children in an environment for proper life training and essential maturity. Unfortunately, **there is not a big effort on discovery of passion and natural abilities.** A great deal of religious instruction is given when our knowledge and intellect are not matured sufficiently to absorb and understand. We take on work that is nothing but a chore and means to money to pay for the commitments undertaken as society suggests and tacitly demands. We make big mistakes and place ourselves in a life that we are not ready to participate or that satisfy our passion and natural abilities. Not all, but most follow this behavior. They are stuck! Somewhere along the way, they feel pressure and the stress, but just do not know what or why. Later they mature and start to discover the dragon. Yes, they are stuck in responsibility and habit that they were not designed or prepared. Do they need help? Well, that's where bullet bob world may be of help. **bullet bob world is** needed to be there early in life, but never too late for the journey to self realization! You are it! You got brain power! Maybe you will unstuck yourself, and maybe you will not. Tuff choice! Kind of scary to think for yourself and more scary to act. Let the hero in you emerge. Discover your passion. Go beyond the self-imposed limits. Live the life that you were designed. Transcend ego, desire and fear. Quit looking to the sky and elsewhere for help. Go within. Use your brain, think, meditate, for everything in the world is there. I know that is a hard assignment. Don't expect perfection. **Do the work!! You can do it!!**

bullet bob presents his world with a writing style combining the simplistic with the abstract. His aim is to connect with everybody that can read or perhaps listen to his low-fog-index communication style. It is not directed to any specific group, educational level, race, religion, nationality, political persuasion or any other division of world society. bullet bob writing can be spiritual, factual, controversial, poetic, critical, compassionate, simple, abstract, informative and inspirational . Yes, all at the same time. Like being in a school room, church, living room, street corner, town meeting, internet café, movie theater or library, all at the same time. As you read you will get to know bullet bob, and just maybe you will discover a little bullet bob in you. **Maybe you will be inspired to write your world.** And as bullet bob reads **your world**, he will surely discover a little **your world** in bullet bob.

THE EIGHT PILLARS ARE

NOBODY KNOWS   Is there an afterlife? What is the purpose of life? What is the size of the universe? Is there a God? Answers to these questions are The Mystery of man. Theology and all other science struggle to solve The Mystery. We do have many theories and we do have faith. We need to know, but actually, nobody knows. If we knew the answers, would there be faith?

Answers to The Mystery are unthinkable, for the truth transcends human thought. The Mystery is beyond today's imagination. Can man's brain focus to a place before the concepts of time, space, and the world of opposites?

Like food and air, man requires spiritual belief. Within the human brain is a section devoted to spirituality. Does the eternal spirit reside there, and do all feel the need to mature the spiritual part of the brain? Without spiritual development and religion, mankind as we know it now, could not function. Mankind would be in mental free fall in a state of absolute chaos manifested in total physical collapse.   Without God's gift of comfort when misfortune strikes, it would be a living hell and perhaps no reason to participate in this earthly journey. What a paradox! We have no choice, so keep the faith brother and sister. Hold on to your religion. Keep the faith! Some say that they are atheist or agnostic, but although hidden to society I believe there is some sort of spiritual belief system to satisfy that eternal spirit within.

Since the beginning of mankind, there has been religion. Religious rites are practiced to satisfy the eternal spirit, establish a faith system of the mystical, to help us mature and maintain our morals and ethics, to assist us thru life's passages, to provide a social order, and to keep you in harmony with the cosmos. Can society exist without religion?

Parable of the Poison Arrow

What about life? Heaven? Hell? Death?   Well, searching for these answers is like a   man shot by a poison arrow. Before allowing others to remove the arrow he wants to know who, why, and what kind of poison? He will die before these questions are answered!

ALL SHARE NATURAL MORALS AND ETHICS   Everybody was and is born with the seed of identical moral and ethical standards. These morals and ethics are elementary ideas programmed in the psyche of all mankind regardless of time and place on earth. Like everything about life, morals and ethics require time to mature. How unfortunate! Can moral maturity be accelerated? I say, yes!

Your parents, teachers, government and clergy share in this huge job to help us mature our natural moral and ethics system. When you violate this system, there is an automatic SIGNAL that you feel.   You know what I am talking about!   However, because of the maturity factor, do each of us experience signals to a different level of morals and ethics?

Because of greed we choose to violate our natural morals and ethics thinking we can get away with it without others knowing. However, you do not fool your psyche, who is judge and punisher. Is that the God within?   In mysterious ways you ALWAYS pay for the violations. The self punishment is some level of hell. Yes, right here on earth.

Although separated by centuries and oceans, all religions are founded on the same basic moral and ethical structure. As society evolves and becomes more complicated likewise moral and ethical interpretations are more complicated. These new interpretations may differ between religions as well as within a given religion. Often there is emotional disagreement, and sometimes there is war. How can this be? Often a new denomination or sect of a given religion is created. Religion is powerful stuff. Too bad that twisted interpretations of morals and ethics are created by greed of the righteous. Human rights and material value issues evoke serious religious disagreement.

Religious and governmental institutions have a habit of twisting morals and ethics to fit their agenda. They preach and propagandize to gain and maintain their power. Often they use tactics to keep us divided. Seldom do they provide accurate or all the information. That is, often lie and tell only what they want you to believe. Perhaps each self-brainwashed. Our way is the best and the only way! Does that sound familiar? They keep the constituents ignorant of other ways and means. Where there is power, there is corruption. So, we have another paradox here. To survive, the religion and government must twist, must advocate divisiveness, must maintain political power or be crushed by a stronger entity that uses identical power tactics. Politics is a nasty business. Unfortunately, that is the real world. We all pay a huge price for these political inspired violations. Therefore, I suggest that you pay attention to your moral and ethical violation signals and be true to them. But don't be stupid. Be as cunning as possible by understanding the politics, and do your absolute best to avoid conflict with your religious and governing institutions.

The best morals reminder that I know of is from Buddhism. Buddha taught the Four Noble Truths. Number one is that all life is suffering. Number two is suffering stems from ego, desire and fear. Number three is that there is a cure for suffering. Number four is the cure, which includes The Eightfold Path.

A very brief description of the Eightfold Path is the following right way to behave:

Right Understanding	Seek to see things as they really are by experience without personal bias
Right Thought	Approach everything in a spirit of kindness, compassion and harmless to others
Right Speech	Avoid lies, slander, abusive language, speaking to much and gossip. Say nothing hurtful.
Right Action	Do nothing to harm others like stealing, taking of life, destruction or abuse of property. No to adultery and overindulging.
Right Livelihood	Do work helpful to others, and do not work in anything that involves arms, drugs and intoxicants.
Right Effort	Use the middle way. Do not go to extremes and use a sensible level of effort.
Right Mindfulness	Live in the moment being mindful of everything you do.
Right Concentration	Learn to focus your mind. Use meditation to develop a higher level of understanding and consciousness.

IMPECABLE MORALS AND RESPECT IS HEAVEN   The prophets of all major religions point to absolute moral behavior and perfect respect for all things. That includes everything beholding our human senses. Experience the world and meditate to mature the moral system within. Pay attention to those violation signals, and behave accordingly. Those violations pertain to every organic and every inorganic thing that is and was. When you disrespect anything in our natural environment or anything produced by man, that is a violation. So, do unto others as you want others to do unto you. Preserve what nature provides. Preserve with perfect maintenance to everything made by man, even a tooth pick. Use it respectfully to the end of utility, and then recycle it. Get your behavior to that level of obedience and heaven is yours. Yes, right here on earth.

Has this been done? No, not by Jesus, Buddha, Mohammad or any other spiritual or religious model. Can it be done? Anything thinkable is possible. If there is a heaven, I say yes! However, all religions believe man is not capable of perfect behavior. Therefore, we create loving Gods that give humans some slack. For example; a savior, various levels of heaven and hell, and reincarnation. It is estimated the chance of living a perfect moral and ethical life may happen only once in the time it will take Mt. Everest to erode to a plane. So, obey as best you can, and you will get your level of heaven or hell right here on earth. Your choice. Choose right!

 INTEGRATE EXPERIENCE WITH THE POWER WITHIN   To attain higher levels of consciousness and understanding, meditation alone will not get the job done. The food for meditation is experience. Although real personal experience is best, vicarious experience can supplement the process of integrating experience with the power of reason. There seem to be no limit of discovery to this process. Energy and determination are essential. An active individual who has actual worldly experience may attain a higher level of understanding than a monk, who is mostly confined to the walls of a monastery. That is, each doing nearly equal study and meditation.

Some say that experience is the best teacher, but perhaps experience is the only teacher. Experience will lead you to your passion. Then, you really have something special to integrate.

Although difficult our job here on earth is to develop that potential power within. Meditation, or just using our brain to find understanding, requires the experience factor for optimum development of the power within. Structured meditation practice is not essential. Just start thinking about a given subject and let the brain's imagination lead you. Stored within the psyche is the optimum meditation formula. All man-made tangibles and intangibles began with a thought. We dream; we act; we meditate; we dream; we act; we meditate… There is no limit. We mature. The more we discover, the more there is to discover.

Often I ask people who are in the last quarter of life, and especially those experiencing the two-minute warning, what would you have done differently in your life? Many times the answer is that they could have done a better job because they did not live up to their potential. Yes, it is very hard to satisfy your potential when the system sucks you in and others often put you down. I suggest you follow your passion and surround yourself with those that lift you up. Strangely, if people sense you are following your passion, they will give you a helping hand. Unfortunately, they may be stuck in the wasteland and not following their passion.

YOU ARE DEFINED BY COMFORT ZONES   Every aspect of your existence is predetermined by your unique system of comfort zones. That DNA or program resides in every cell of your body. Yes, you have a comfort zone for wealth, sports, body weight, neatness, school grades, social standing, job status and everything about you. You may work your way below or work your way above your unique comfort zone, but more often only to return. We are programmed. How often do we hear things like I could be, should be, will be and would be? Why let ego frustrate yourself? Eliminate the anxiety. The fact is that you are stuck with yourself. Live gracefully in total self-acceptance and be in harmony with what nature gave you. This can provide a beautiful life.

To change our unique comfort zones is a huge challenge, but if driven with passion it is possible. Rigorous discipline and energy are required. Only passion can sustain this journey. This is the hero's journey. The one who dares to challenge the limits? It is a lonely and long journey because you go psychologically where few or no other has been. This is the grail quest.

Perhaps, this suggests it is not wise to try changing the behavior of others. Even when someone requests help to change his or her behavior pattern, the possibility of real and permanent change of habit is slim. No passion, no change. Another paradox evolves. Yes, we must attempt to help others to improve in spite of the poor odds of success. Maybe we try because of compassion, or guilt, or maybe it is the spontaneous realization that we are metaphysically connected. You and I are one!

I once knew a young couple in romantic love. Each had one very bad habit. Each was aware of the other's bad habit. Marriage will change us and that was the cure. Shortly, there was more awareness to bad habits followed by divorce. What is the chance of something like this ever happening? Can you make a silk purse from a sow's ear?

CHOOSE YOU PASSION AS YOUR LIFE'S WORK   You do not have to get trapped by the social system. Following the social system may provide a nice life, but more than likely, that is not what you were programmed to be. That is living a life in conflict with the consciousness of the organs within the body. Yes, mental and physical disease is thus manifested. You are stuck. You are living in the lowest conscious level. Your energies are not being used to discover the power within. Your dragons hold you back, and you know what dragons do. Yes, they hold you back. Dragons live by a cave guarding gold and beautiful maidens, but have no desire or use of either. Identify the social system dragon, find the passion to slay the dragon, and the gold and the beautiful maidens are yours. They are within and always have been.

Never work for the money. You can survive working for a buck for a short time, but do that only in desperation. Find your passion. Follow it, and the material will come naturally.

How do you find your passion? There probably is no absolute scientific formula or method. Keep an open mind. Be active and experience the world. Just can't get enough of it attitude. Be like the happy Buddha, who is in total enjoyment in the sorrows of the world. Take risks by breaking the rules of society, but don't be foolish and violate the moral system within. Be a hero. Go, do and think like no other. When you experience your passion, you will recognize it. Your consciousness will transcend ego, desire and fear.

FEEL COMFORTABLE WITH ALL RELIGIONS   Learn as much as you can about the world's religions. Visit churches, temples, mosques, and other holy places. Participate in the rituals if allowed. By participating in the services and other rituals you can receive the message. The ritual (music) may be different, but the message (word) is almost the same. Do unto others as … and behave in accord with the universal moral and ethical law. To get the most from the ritual study is required, but without study you can feel the message informing your subconscious while your conscious is in transformation. However, if you are aware of the history of the religion and the symbolic meaning of the rites, you may have an awesome mystical experience.

Enter any holy building from a busy street and you will feel a huge transformation of consciousness. Your thoughts become quiet and morally awakened. You may be overwhelmed and feel a connection to the divine. When exiting the holy place you return to the busy street awaiting transformation back to the competitive world. Back to doing what is necessary to survive in the complicated man-made rules of the business world. Often these tainted rules are reinvented, changed and twisted at an alarming rate. Often they violate the natural morals and ethics within. This is serious internal conflict. Get me to a psychiatrist. Give me a pill. Give me a drink. Somebody help me. Oh, if I could only quit, but I'm stuck in the system. The system is the trap, with money as the bait! I must pay the mortgage, the car loans, kids braces. Thank God my wife works. Maybe I'll get some sex tonight. Hope she's not tired. Well, Sunday I'll be back to church. I'll be centered for at least an hour or two!

What a price to pay for being trapped by the system. Just can't wait to get home. Weekends and holidays are what I live for. Gee, I'll have a lot of money when I retire, but I'm only 25 years old. Only 40 years, and I can retire from this work. You know that I live in the greatest country on earth. My parents do this and are a great example, so why should I be different?

Yes, yes, yes! Be different. Say no to the wasteland. Say no to the system. Live in the moment! Live in rapture! Live in bliss! Live in your passion!

THE GRAND IDEAL IS WHEN

When the vast majority of mankind truly believes that we are all one connected by universal mater, energy and consciousness. We are all brothers and sisters of Mother Earth, for that's where we evolved.

When the vast majority of mankind shed their ignorance by learning world religions and beholds unity.

When the masses say no to violent behavior and war. When the powerful promote immoral and unethical behavior, and the masses say no.

When it is politically correct to talk about religion, politics, sex and all controversial topics with a spirit of learning and respect and without malice.

When the vast majority of people are following their passion. When mankind is discovering the unlimited power within, for everything in the universe resides within all beings.

When society's goals are in concert with the unlimited power within the individual, evoking a resonate effect on man's endeavor to discover the universe and unveil The Mystery. When mankind is thus challenged, war on this planet is history!

When new challenges transcend the imagination of man. Yes, when man progresses to that place that transcends time, space, and the world of opposites. When man goes beyond the unthinkable.

Perhaps, there will be a cold day in hell!

What's this all about bullet bob?   Is there purpose and meaning in life?

Well, let me tell you in rhyme.

Flying down life's path, where did I go?
The choices were endless and so,
But now in a glide on this mysterious ride,
Where will it end?
I guess I'll just blend.
Dead hand to sand,
Starry eye to sky,
Net worth back to earth, and so forth.

Ah! But memories survive,
And that's why you're alive,
To create them!
So, when angels look back on my memory track,
Like a clinging vine,
Those very special moments when,
Your memory track, meets mine!....

Speak to me bullet, Speak to me. You are a very special dog! Do you know that?

No, but what did you expect?   After all, I am man's best friend. Kindness is my
vision.

Are you a God?

Maybe! Are we Gods? Are all of us Gods?   Are we The Mystery? Can we fit on a cross?
 Can we sit in lotus position?   Can we transcend ego, desire and fear?

Oh, Yes, Yes, WE ARE! And, Oh Yes, Yes, WE CAN!!

Is this new stuff, bullet bob?

Maybe? At least relatively new in terms of the planet Earth's age.   I'd estimate this stuff is
at least 8,000 years old .

Really? Yes, really.

You are shit'n me. Why didn't I hear about it?

Suggest you read this again. The answer is within.

by bullet bob   ON BEING   October 6th, 2008

Did you ever think about being? What is this thing called being? Can you describe being? Well, let's meditate on being. Yes, use some mental energy to explore this mysterious phenomena of being.

BEING MAY BE MORE THAN CONSCIOUSNESS. Human consciousness is the ability to feel, see, hear, smell and taste. These are physical sensors that feed the brain and other organs of the body which intern perform their unique function. The brain is agile and can process these signals from the sensors. It can reason, memorize and initiate action. Also, there are involuntary responses that are programmed before birth and others by habit. These signals may have impact on the emotions such as euphoria, anger, sadness which manifest smiles, aggression and depression. Man has the ability to experience a myriad of emotions; we should experience and accept all of them as affirmation that we are alive. Some have better control of emotions via experience, and maybe that is a sign of maturity or fear of showing their human side. The more the sensors experience the better we process the signals. We learn to reason better. We learn to memorize better. We mature our morals and ethics. We create wisdom. We make better choices in our behavior and relationships. We improve our state of being. The limits of understanding, wisdom and consciousness may be infinite.

We have a fair understanding of this mechanical aspect of human consciousness, but what about the spiritual? What about the soul? Yes, those are a huge aspect of being, for this is the ultimate mystery. Although nobody really knows, the possible explanations just may be the most powerful things on this earth. Yes, we are talk'en spirituality and religion!

ALL LIVING THINGS HAVE CONSCIOUSNESS.   That includes everything in the Animal and Plant Kingdoms. Notice how plants grow toward sun light and water. How is that taught? Notice how animals stalk and choose their food. Is that taught? All living organisms survive by devouring other living organisms. How about that for innate consciousness? It's a cruel world!

There are an infinite number of living organisms on this earth and they have very simple conscious systems to the very complex with human beings as the most advances and sophisticated. Are there different levels of human consciousness? Of course there are, but do we have equal ability to attain higher levels of consciousness? Is there pure consciousness? That is something to argue.

Does the inorganic on this planet have a conscious? After all, they are made of the same elements and universal energy as the organic. If so, there is universal connection that suggests respect. Is that universal energy God? Man's original deities were Gods of nature. Powerful Gods of nature like Sun, Moon, Fire, Water, and Wind were common. There is Mother Nature. If there is universal energy, there must be universal consciousness. We have gravity, and is it not a form of consciousness?

THE SOUL IS INVISIBLE, TASTELESS, ODORLESS, AND CANNOT BE HEARD   Does the soul have sensors? Are there other dimensions of communication and consciousness? Do we not have intuition and the metaphysical? Saint Paul wrote that our soul shall live in our spiritual body in the hereafter. How does the soul operate and communicate? Intuition is powerful, and don't we wish we connect better and have absolute trust in it? There must be unknown connectors and sensors. We must find a way to discover and define them in our quest to better understand being, the soul and the mystic. Today man is not mentally equipped to give a finite explanation of the soul.   We try. The soul is part of the great mystery which today transcends human thought.

BE THE BEST BEING THAT YOU CAN BE   Should that be man's ultimate goal here on earth? Well, that goal is not easy, and just maybe this test on earth was not designed to be easy. To improve our level of consciousness takes time, hard work, and patience. First we must become aware of and mature our morals and ethics. In concert we develop the power of reason. Early in life our parents provide the guidance by using discipline and place you in an environment that provides the proper experience necessary to mature morals, improve the power of reason, gather knowledge, and sharpen the intellect. With the help of clergy, schoolteachers, police, and community your parents gradually pass the maturity process over to you. After twenty or so years, you are now in charge of this never ending maturity process. Society imposes a huge number of rules, regulations directives of significant complication to struggle with. This is the beginning of a tuff job and maybe it just isn't fair. After all, you didn't ask for this job. Life is a struggle, and maybe later on in this journey you will learn that it is necessary. STRUGGLE is the VITALITY of LIFE. You can give up and decay, or decide to terminate this visit. I say take charge, compete and enjoy the struggle. Enjoy the game. You will score. You have four quarters and maybe overtime. You will win. You are born with the winning plays. Now, go within and discover them.

BEING IS AN INFINITE NUMBER OF MID-COURSE CORRECTIONS   No one obeys their moral system perfectly. Each violation removes us off the heavenly path. We then pay the punishment to get back on track. The punishment comes in some form of stress, and the amount is a function of violation seriousness. The punishment is some level of hell. Yes, right here on earth.

 How does one know when one is in moral or ethical violation? There is a signal that you feel. Pay attention to it! Violations create stress and stress may manifest itself in physical disease. If you are not eating well, sleeping well, thinking well or relating with others well, best you take time out to identify the violation and make the correction. Society is one big huge moral and ethical violation trap. So, how many mid-course corrections did you do this week? Did you say your prayers?

THE BEING OF ALL BEINGS WAS THE FIRST BEING   His first thought was I, which was the beginning of ego. His second thought was a need for company, which was the beginning of desire. His third thought was death, which was the beginning of fear. Henceforth all beings suffer as victims of ego, desire and fear. The goal of being is to eliminate ego, desire and fear. The desire to perform this goal in itself is a desire. You must find your individual way to eliminate the ego, desire and fear without a desire to eliminate them. That is quite a trick, but if it is thinkable, it is possible. You will then transform your consciousness to that place before the being of all beings, time, space, and the world of opposites. Then perhaps unveil the mystery of being.

To survive on this planet one need not eliminate ego, desire and fear, but learn to use them wisely. Without them mankind cannot improve or exist. So, as in Hindu tradition, the elimination of ego, desire and fear is reserved for the later stage of life. This is the final stage of the maturity process. How many, if any, have attained ultimate maturity before exit? I say only a few. After all, do we not live predominately in a society of adolescence? Perhaps few have eliminated ego, desire and fear. Gutama, the first Buddha, did it and called it Enlightenment, but did he unveil the mystery of being?

bullet bob is human consciousness part of the soul?

Yes, I think so. I suspect that consciousness, soul and spirit are linked in a strong relationship, but the relationship is currently beyond my awareness. There are infinite kinds and levels of consciousness that reside in the mind. Mankind struggles with this difficult to control monkey brain as it swings randomly from thought to thought. The mind has ability to navigate all sorts and levels of consciousness, and sometimes get stuck or totally unrestrained. The goal is to train the mind to produce thoughts and subsequent behavior acceptable to societal acceptance. This is a complicated tuff job because society is dynamic and conflicted. One tool, to keep mind and body healthy, is meditation. Meditation is a topic upcoming in this document.

bullet bob why psychiatrists?

I believe their job is to make aware and assist people the ability to properly take charge of their mind power. Often using the practice of indirect counseling, the patient makes connection with their brain power to identify the dragon and slay it. That is, identify the problem and fix it with their own ability to rationalize. Psychiatrist job is to find and slay dragons. The technique used by psychiatrists varies by person, and that is a tuff assignment. Many expensive sessions with no guarantee. Sometimes mission impossible and sometimes addictive. Such a job!

 bullet bob are you being?

Yes. Isn't everything some form of being? Universal consciousness is the great connector.

bullet bob are you confused?

Yes and no. You see I'm a dog. Special, but I am a dog. Let me tell you a story. Once upon a time a man made a wooden dog and placed it on the lawn. One day I spotted that wooden dog. So naturally I smelled it, then bit it, then lifted my leg to leak on it.

bullet bob what's that story all about?

For the most part I live by my natural dog instinct and philosophy. That is: If you can't fuck it, and you can't eat it, PISS on it!

bullet bob shame on you.

I'm so sorry. I'm so confused and frustrated because the mystery of being is within and I can't make connection with it. Am I the mystery, and that's why I keep chasing my tail?

But what is a hero? There are all kinds of heroes. One kind is someone that thinks and acts like no other in the quest of a noble deed. That is behaving and performing beyond the limits of your comfort zone, the life you were programmed and societies boundaries. One can attain the highest levels of consciousness and understanding by meditating the hero's journey experience with the deepest power of the psyche's imagination. The hero's journey is a psychological as well as a physical one. The psychological is the emotional high. The physical is the perfect functioning of the organs that thrive and make possible the survival of the journey. When your senses are alive and all of the organs of the body are working perfectly, and only then you know you are on the hero's journey.

Does the hero choose the journey? Do you plan the journey? Yes and no. The hero's journey is the one he is ready for. One just feels the need! The need feeling is the hero's call. Perhaps, it is the call to your passion. You are living a life that you were not designed, and you feel the need to find your passion which hopefully is the hero's journey. Everyone gets the call, but fear gets in the way. The trick is not to eliminate fear, but learn to use it wisely. After all, the hero may walk the razor's edge and risks the winds that can blow you off balance to terminate the journey. Fear keeps the senses at a peak to combat the threatening terminal winds. The heightened level of awareness is the high and the joy, however no need to worry for there is always a helping hand. Others, although stuck in the social system, will sense that you are following your passion, the hero's journey, and will always give the support that you need.

Although the goal is the journey's end, there is sure to be a letdown. Yes, nothing is permanent. If you want to maintain the high, the passion, the quest, you must seek a new hero journey. The absence of the quest is to give up and await decay. First a spiritual decay, then physical decay terminated by life's exit. After all, the hero's journey keeps your body organs happy and work at peak performance. Unhappy organs deteriorate. So, be a hero to keep them happy. Act on the call and walk the razor's edge! Live in rapture. Live longer.

Maybe this explains why the young men in military service to protect our country are proud, happy and physically function so well. Often they unknowingly are thrust into the hero's journey. Yes, totally unaware of the transformation. When leaving military service often to decay and live only in the memory. Unfortunately, they may never be aware of the need of a new journey, never aware of the inner power to create a new journey, never to act on the call. What a waste. How sad.

To reach a higher level of consciousness, all of us must use energy to develop the brain's potential power. Learn to think for yourself and prepare for the hero's call. Let others think for you and you are stuck in the wasteful social system. You can survive at this lower level of consciousness, but you give up the joy, the high, your life, and sink into the wasteland. The wasteland is the void between what you achieved and the higher level of achievement, joy and understanding that you are capable.

To prepare it is important to search for the right thoughts for the mind to process. That is right mindfulness. Yes, right thinking is work. Use your energy to experience everything that you possibly can. Don't be afraid of the new, and fill your mind with new experience. The mind is programmed and naturally selects from the experience to provide right mindfulness. Use meditation. Instruction on how to meditate is helpful, but not necessary. Just do it! Get the experience, and trust the power within for there the optimum meditation formula resides. Yes, integrate the experience with the power of the minds intellect. You will be on your way to higher levels of awareness and consciousness. You may discover your passion. You will be ready for the call. This is the first step to the hero's journey.

bullet bob, why be a hero?

Maybe it gives meaning and purpose to life, and everyone adores the hero and his adventurous journey.

bullet bob, can I be a hero?

Of course you can! Perhaps by happen stance, by design, or by choice. But, really makes no difference how. Prepare for the call. Then, just do it!

bullet bob, I have responsibility like a job, wife, kids.

Maybe they can be included in your hero's journey, and maybe they can't. Tuff decision!! The Buddha left his wife and child upon the call, and later returned after enlightenment.

bullet bob, are you a hero?

. Maybe! Sometimes I think I'm the message, and sometimes I think I'm the Messenger. **Serious warning**, stop that kind of thinking!

MY PARENTS TOLD ME TO USE MY HEAD   What did they mean by that? I suppose they meant to think before I did something stupid. Yes, use my brain, and I didn't need further instruction. Was that a clue to the power of the brain? I believe everyone meditates all the time including sleep. Today meditation is suggested. I imagine structured conscious meditation is some sort of spiritual, relaxation or physical yoke exercise. Within religion there are rites of structured meditation like prayer, chant, singing, and body language to create divine experience and emotional tranquility. Scientists deal with how structured meditation effects brain chemistry and impact on mental health, physical health and human behavior. Brain power may be infinite and continues to expand as the human being continues to progress. I suggest you go to your computer and type the word "meditation" in the GOOGLE box. There will be a variety of discussion on the types, uses and definition of meditation. Far too many to discuss in this writing, and way beyond my knowledge.

THE MIND HAS A MIND OF IT'S OWN   I recollect from Hinduism many years ago the mind was compared to a monkey that swings from thought to thought randomly and non-stoppable. It's like a car radio in search mode with no ability to stop the search or turn it off. Can you predict your dreams? Many forms of meditation are designed to stop brain activity, but I doubt if any succeeded. In quest to mature and focus our thought process we struggle to develop an ability to efficiently use this out-of-control tool called the brain. This is a tuff assignment and what is produced in this quest is an infinite variety of thoughts and consciousness. Yes, all do not share identical experience or method to obtain knowledge or level of consciousness. Consequently, all humanity is unique and unfortunately there is **conflict.** Human beings are most interesting, but probably the most dangerous thing on planet earth.

 THE ENTIRE UNIVERSE RESIDES IN THE HUMAN BRAIN   Are we the mystery? Potentially everything that exists in the universe is within the ultimate power of the human brain. How can that be, for all of us evolve from the tiniest of tiniest particle of matter? Beyond our imagination the infinite small contains infinite ability. A task beyond imagination, but collective humanity on this earth, and maybe beyond, will evolve super humans of infinite physical and mental abilities. All this from practically nothing! In my short lifetime humans have made significant improvements in physical and mental abilities. Records of all human abilities have been shattered, and that phenomenon will continue eternally. Can mankind accelerate the super human development process? Yes, but the battle between progress and evil is eternal. Unfortunately, on this earth and in the universe there is good vs. evil, right vs. wrong, superior vs. inferior, or the universe of opposites. Fortunately, humanity continues to move slowly to good, right, and superior. The journey is long and so difficult, but super humanity will evolve and evolve. Are we a link in the chain of **the mystery? Do you believe in "Superman"**

YOU ARE AS YOU THINK   If you are to consciously meditate, that is, take time from you busy work and play schedule, to seek higher levels of understanding, concentration, awareness, contentment, achievement and consciousness, I suggest that you focus your mind on positive thoughts. If you wish to be relaxed, achieve divine experience, be loved, be beautiful, be healthy, be smart or anything imaginable, just go within. That is, get in touch with the power of the brain via meditation. The efficient meditative formula resides in your mind, but if you wish to use a mantra, beads, posture, prayer, chant, incense, darkness, or whatever to put your mind in a meditative state. That's ok. Just do it! Find your way to connect with the power of the brain. As long as your meditative thoughts and desires are within the boundaries of reasonable morals, ethics, common sense and **maybe** physical science (since we could be dealing with the unknown and supernatural), they are achievable. However, there is work involved, for you do not get something for nothing. Yes, you must work to keep the mind and body on the prescription found thru the meditative process. Maybe miracles, but they must be earned. Choice always prevails. Remember "if it's thinkable, it is possible". Limits can be transcended.

bullet bob, what is kundalini yoga?

Wow, I know little and never experienced. I believe kundalini yoga is type of meditation originated in India by a few branches of Hinduism over 2200 years ago. It has been called by many names and technique varies throughout the ages. Kundalini is a more modern term for a symbolic rite that uses a breath control method to move the kundalini, a coiled snake, located at the base of the spine upward to the skull. The breathing pattern creates energy to move the kundalini upward to visit seven levels of consciousness called chakras.

LEVEL	LOCATION	CONSCIOUS FOCUS	PRINCIPALS
1	Base	Basic life requirements	Uninspired, low creative
2	Sex Organs	Sex	Fruedians (everyone)
3	Belly	Competition, Violence	Politicians, Businessmen
4	Heart	Compassion	Jesus, Buddha
5-7	Head	Devine	Spiritual Devotees

The vast majority attain level 4, however the majority dwell oscillating levels 1-3. I do not believe it requires structured meditation to operate on those first three levels, but often individuals get stuck in one of them. Level 4, compassion, may require some sort of structured meditative practice to dwell there. Levels 5-7 require massive doses of structured meditation, and if not a monk or yogi, perhaps retired people. Keep in mind that kundalini yoga is a symbolic educational rite, but there are those who do serious practice.

bullet bob, do you meditate?

Yes and no!   I am guilty of right mindfulness for the most part, but the work or right action is far from perfection. I go around meditating all the time, and to many people I appear slow to react which may cause relationship problems. Especially when I express underlying analysis. Perhaps I may appear in a very different realm of consciousness or out of this world.

bullet bob, do you do structured meditation?

Yes and no! I say prayer at bedtime followed by focus on subjects that I feel a need for understanding and guidance. I then review today's past action, think about that action, then plan on tomorrow's quest. I try to be insightful, moral and ethical in thought, speech and actions as I navigate this earthly challenge. I search the internet for information, read books, study, watch educational and newsworthy TV, travel, welcome new experience and test my current opinion by conversation. I ask questions about important subjects, but often no answers.

Bullet bob, why do you write?

Why not? I call it written meditation. Once I begin to write I am often amazed what is written. Where did that come from? Maybe the subconscious knows! Maybe others have had the same experience when composing thoughts? I have no lock on creativity! Hey, slight chance someone will read this meditative dissertation.

YOU CREATE YOUR VERY OWN GOD   Because you have a brain and a mind you have the ability to design and build a God of your choice. Scientists say that embedded in the human brain is a unique section devoted to spirituality. Is that evidence of God existence? Is that where your spiritual sensor resides? Although society will have influence on the God that you create, the seed of God planted within the spirituality section of the brain will have the ultimate influence on the makeup of your God creation. Spirituality is a maturing process. That suggests that your God is ever changing just as everything in the universe is in constant change. The rate of change is a function of worldly experience and meditation on God. Can God creation be accelerated? Of course, it is a function of effort and the quality of spiritual environment that you reside. Is there an end to this God creation process? Maybe never, but as your God creation matures it will more resemble that of your neighbors and ultimately unite as one true God creation. Yes, the God seed planted in you is identical to that planted for maturity in all. Has the absolute God maturity ever happened? Yes, but oh so few, for there are a multitude of survival and pleasurable actions competing during this earthly journey.

GOOD NEWS - YOU GET THE GOD THAT YOU CREATE   That suggests that you create wisely, and also devote sufficient time and effort. Study of the many Eastern, Western and Native Religions is very helpful, but the search thru meditation is absolutely necessary to discover the God seed within. The object is to discover your very own path to inner peace, joy and salvation. Following the path of others may be and easier task and work for you, but creating your very own unique path can provide greater joy, passion and intensity of divine consciousness.

A HUGE COMPONENT OF GOD CREATION IS MORALS AND ETHICS DEVELOPMENT
This may be the most challenging and complicated creation effort, because of conflict with politics and laws of the society in which you live. Also, if your moral and ethical code is too pure, your societal behavior to survive may cause constant violation of your conscious with subsequent self-punishment of a living hell. A very low-level of morals and ethics may cause violation of societies laws and ethics which isolate you like in jail or people wish not to associate with you. So, it is wise to not be extreme in moral and ethical code. Be gracious. Take the middle path, but unfortunately you do the work of navigator. Good luck! Keep in mind that society, by human design, is a huge moral and ethics violation trap!

YOUR GOD CREATION MAY CONCIST OF THE FOLLOWING QUALITIES

- A loving God of compassion and forgiveness
- A just God not preoccupied with judgment and harsh punishment
- A just God that rewards good behavior
- A powerful God of infinite supernatural abilities
- A God that is everywhere always

- A God that transcends thought and beyond the limits of time, space and the world of opposites
- A God that listens and answers prayers
- A God that gives comfort in times of misfortune
- A God that assists and allows me to find and be the God within
- A God that helps me see the divinity in all creatures
- A God that guides me to respect to all and everything in the universe and beyond
- A God that provides guidance in the participation of joy and pleasure
- A God that gives special power to do onto others as I wish others to do unto me
- A God that expects me to continually improve my insight, knowledge and wisdom
- A God that helps me find my unique spiritual path and show respect for the path of others
- A God that recognizes evil and by constant reminder to avoid.
- An ever maturing God that is in concert with science and societal progress

bullet bob, does everyone create a God?

Yes, for everyone of sound mind. As a minimum God, all create a system of morals and ethics. For those of unsound mind, I can only speculate a more simplistic but efficient God creation. Let us expand by saying that all creatures of the universe feel the spirit and in some unique way create and respond.

bullet bob, can you define God?

I struggle with definition, because God is beyond my current brain power. I just feel the spirit.

bullet bob, Is God a person, pure consciousness, an illusion, a spirit, a moral and ethics system, or universal energy?

God may be all that and more. Nobody really knows. God has no boundaries. God is everywhere but yet nowhere. God is known, but unknown. God transcends mass, time and space. God is a metaphor; the mystic focus of religious superstition.

bullet bob, how do I know of this mystery?

Well, just turn on your spiritual sensor! Really ain't all that difficult!

by bullet bob   ABOUT MORALS AND ETHICS (M&E)   17 June 2011

ARE SEEDS OF M&E PLANTED BY BIRTH?

IS IT A PRIMARY FUNCTION OF FAMILY AND RELIGION TO HELP DEVELOP YOUR M&E AND REMIND YOU TO OBEY?

HOW DOES YOUR SOCIAL ENVIRONMENT HAVE IMPACT ON M&E DEVELOPMENT?

IS THERE A "RIGHT" KNOWLEDGE IN M&E DEVELOPMENT?

IS MEDITATION NECESSARY TO INTEGRATE EXPERIENCE WITH INTELECT FOR M&E DEVELOPMENT?

IS IT NECESSARY TO BUILD A STRONGER AWARENESS OF M&E VIOLATION?

DOES YOUR M&E STANDARDS AND OBEYANCE AUTOMATICALLY IMPROVE WITH AGE?

IS THERE A STANDARD OF M&E BY AGE?

CAN M&E SYSTEM DEVELOPMENT BE ACCELERATED? CAN IT BE REVISED?

DOES THE ABSENCE OF M&E AVOID GUILT?

IS MATURITY OF YOUR M&E BEHAVIOR IS A PRIME FUNCTION OF BEING?

IF YOUR M&E STSTEM CREATES YOUR HEAVEN OR HELL, IS IT WISE TO PERFECT YOUR M&E SYSTEM?

DOES THE JUDGE WITHIN SERVE SELF PUNISHMENT USING YOUR CURRENT LEVEL OF M&E AWARENESS?

IF THERE IS A GOD, IS GOD THE FINAL JUDGE?

IF GOD IS YOUR M&E SYSTEM, DO YOU CREATE YOUR OWN GOD?

SHOULD GOD REQUIRE EACH OF US TO DEVELOP AND OBEY OUR M&E TO A SPECIFIC STANDARD?

SHOULD GOD CONSIDER THE LEVEL OF M&E STANDARDS DEVELOPMENT WHEN GIVING PUNISHMENT FOR VIOLATION?

IS "DO UNTO OTHERS AS YOU WANT THEM TO DO UNTO YOU" A FUNDAMENTAL FOUNDATION FOR M&E SYSTEM DEVELOPMENT?

bullet bob,   why did you present this writing in the form of questions?

Well, I thought this would be an experiment in writing style, and perhaps turn on the reader imagination.

bullet bob do you have answers to these questions?

Yes I have answers today, but tomorrow I may have better answers. That is, if I pay attention to my Jiminy Cricket! And by the way, he just won't stop preaching!! Is there an end to his wisdom?

bullet bob   can you define morals and ethics?

I will try. Simply stated as your actions and speech should not cause hurt, harm, suffering or negative impact in any way to all nature on this planet earth and beyond by intent and otherwise.

bullet bob   can you define nature?

Nature is all living and non-living matter which exists in the universe.

bullet bob   what is intent all about?

Well, if a person's morals and ethics have not matured to the level of an action or speech violation, it may be unintentional, but still a violation. Inexperience and ignorance may or may not be punishable. Should a baby be punished for excessive crying? Should a speeding driver be arrested if unaware of the speed limit? Should a soldier be punished for doing the duty of killing or injuring the enemy?

bullet bob   this is getting complicated!

Yes, yes! So do your best to improve your moral and ethics and pay attention to those violation signals. Take a common sense approach like be mindful before you act or speak, and improve your sensitivity to society's written and unwritten law as best you can. Be careful, for society is one huge moral and ethics violation trap! Good luck!

by bullet bob   CREATION   24 November 2012

CREATURES BY DESIGN CREATE   Everything is the universe and beyond is at work
doing the duty of creation. All entities and creatures everywhere participate because anything
created contains the inherent ability to create along with a natural desire and perhaps a **duty.**
Thus, everything in the universe and beyond is in constant change because creation has no
boundaries at any level. Although the creative process is inherent, but what is created is of
random generation. This may be by virtue of concepts such as **free will** and **choice** as spoken in
religions and spirituality. Prediction of past and future creation, so far, is current practice, but
nowhere near an exact science.

TIME AND SPACE DIMENSIONS OF CREATION ARE A MYSTERY   How big is the
universe? Are there multiple universes? Is there a smallest particle of matter? How does
vibrant energy form mass? Are there other dimensions beyond time and space? Is there a
beginning to time, space, energy and matter? Everyday scientists are at work to create new
technology to discover answers to these questions. Is there an architect that started this creation
process? This may take ions to solve! Maybe never solved!

EVERYTHING EVERYWHERE IS IN CONSTANT CHANGE   Nothing is permanent
except the creation process. Look, listen, feel, smell and taste to verify that all we experience is
bound by time and space. Everything we experience has a life span. Some exist only a fraction
of a second while others last beyond our imagination, but all participate in the cycle of birth and
death. Do dreams occupy space and participate in life-death cycle? If it is thinkable, it is
possible! The great mystery of mankind is the possibility of a describable source that put this
creative process into motion. But, why? What's it all about? Some say that God knows, but
there is serious disagreement of a God concept.

CREATION MAY BE PRE-DERTIMINED   Is the universe with it's infinite components and
actions the product of a master plan? Are you and I actors in an enormous complicated plot?
Or maybe our destiny is an illusion as we act out the dreams of an almighty source? All on this
planet dream and act on many of our dreams, and we all participate in the dreams of others.
There are little dreams, big dreams and maybe all interconnected by the master dream. Do our
thoughts and action do have universal impact? No one really knows, but we do know the
thought or dream is the universal driving force of the creation process shared by all, and that may
include the almighty source. So, we now have a dilemma about this concept of **choice.**

bullet bob, is there divine creation?

Yes, it is everywhere!   Some call it Religious masturbation. Think about that!

 bullet bob, about creation, dreams, imagination and illusion; are we just play actors in this earthly drama? Is this concept of free will and choice a problem?

Well, think of people as eternal children playing imaginary games. We play many roles on this journey and often never show or discover true self. Picture a military general sitting next to the president with a uniform filled with stars and metals. He is playing defender of our nation although probably never experienced front-line duty, and the guy next to him is playing congressman, a politician, who has never done an honest day of labor in his entire life. Think about the man who sings in the church quire on Sunday as an angel, and after services is selling a life insurance policy to an eighty-year old millionaire. Look at the guy attired in black with white collar playing agent of Jesus teaching and later molests a young boy. What about a young man in veteran hospital with loss of limb; a victim of political role players. Do we ever grow up to honest human realization and abandon the masquerade? I remember a story told by the late Joseph Campbell about driving into town and parking his auto. Upon getting out of the auto a little boy was standing on the curb and said to Joseph, "You cannot park there". "Why not", replied Joseph. "Because I am a fire hydrant" the boy informed. Well, what will be the next role for that little boy; maybe someday a CEO of a major corporation. So, why go to the movies when each and every day we are surrounded by potential academy award winners!!

bullet bob, does everything dream?

If there is universal consciousness and creation, I say yes!

bullet bob, how can non-living non-organic dream?

Although I am a very wise dog, I really can't explain, but my intuition says, yes! If you do not trust me, use your power within. You may be the next Einstein, but be prepared for a struggle beyond imagination.

WHAT IS RELIGION?   It is not so easy to define, and perhaps difficult for scholars to agree. The work "religion" is derived from Latin "religio" to bind. I surmise that refers partly to the participation in rituals. My simplistic definition of Religion is a belief system of faith in the mystic, and with emphasis on the word "system".

RELIGION OR FAITH SYSTEMS CONSIST OF COMMON FUNCTIONS

- An explanation of the mystic
- Guidance in morals and ethics development
- Assistance with life's milestones
- A social structure and program

AN EXPLANATION OF THE MYSTIC   That is provide answers to universal questions such as: What happens after death? Universe creation? How did man originate? A creator? These and other questions are the mystic or "The Great Mystery" of mankind. Regarding this mystical belief, the word "truth" seems to be a common theme with all sorts of explanation of why this particular faith is the one and only "truth". Most religion seems to twist, probe, reinterpret scripture and in constant discovery to defend their version of "truth".

Because man has and always had the need, stronger than desire, to satisfy this mystic quest, he will participate in a religion. The answers or "truth" of the mystic is the bait, and the rituals are the hook. The hooks are frightfully effective and often sharpened to fit the current culture changes and scientific knowledge. If religion does not keep up with society and science, that religion slowly disappears and then is termed "myth". TODAY'S RELIGIONS MAY BE TOMORROW'S MYTHS.

The solution to the Great Mystery for all practical purposes is currently unsolvable because it transcends man's current brain power and imagination. NOBODY KNOWS. However the human need for faith in the mystic resides in the utmost depth of the psyche, and man desperately needs forgiveness and hope or perhaps experience a living hell to death. And I must mention that religion serves as a must needed foundation for the structure and order of civilization and the mythology we live by. So, keep the faith, brother and sister; hold on, hold on to your religion and participate. Feel the spirit. It's there.

Unfortunately, faith always struggles with doubt. How strong is your faith? How strong is your doubt? Regardless, participate in the rites, and receive and behave in accord with the morals and ethics message. Do that and you will satisfy the eternal spirit that is felt by all. Amen.

WORLD RELIGIONS HAVE MUCH IN COMMON   I refer you to the chart on the following page called **Religion Commonality**. There a list of religious belief, ritual and product that are components or the major World Religions. May I point out that many times there was no communication or awareness of other Religions when these common beliefs, rituals, and products were created by religions of unknown world culture. Separated by oceans, other continents were unknown for thousands of years, especially the Americas which were discovered by European adventurers in the 15th century. When European discovered the Aztec society with belief system, temples, ritual similar to Christianity, they were astounded and surely a Christian somehow adventured there before their voyage and help found the Aztec religion. Well, scholars throughout world history suspect that there are elementary ideas, ritual and need for religion wired into all mankind. Especially, they find overwhelming commonality in religious ritual, morals, ethics and story themes. Somewhere in all religions is that common moral and ethical concept called the **golden rule**. **Do unto others as you would want them to do unto you.** That is the foundation of all world religion moral and ethical doctrine as well as secular law. When comparing world religion it does not take too much study to discover the huge amount of commonality, and then you begin to get the notion that all world religion point to a common mystic of supernatural creative power that has all the answers to the mystical questions about the universe creation, life and afterlife. Yes, we are all one in that common quest. So, why all the turmoil, violence, killing and division? Well, when Religion is institutionalized, power is created. Power always creates greed and corruption, and man seems to be flawed because he just can't get enough ego, power and greed. Unfortunately, the Religion is man-made, and as consequence a lot of bad things happen. Yes, the righteous can twist, reinvent and reinterpret scripture to fit their greedy agenda. Amazingly, they get a following due to compelling tactics and a poorly informed audience that are eager for leadership and the need for spiritual guidance. But we must understand that religious institutions do a huge amount of good works, which are presented throughout this discussion.

Why can't all religion preach unity with all other religions? I think I just answered that question! Will man ever grow up? Will man learn to control greed and power addiction? Will man shed ignorance and ego? Not likely. But you as an individual can grow up. May you improve your level of religious understanding and consciousness, and discover religious unity and the true meaning of religious freedom. That will provide individual peaceful existence, and if we all individually improve our understanding of religious freedom, we just may have a good chance of a more peaceful world.

bullet bob, do you feel the spirit?

Yes, I do! I really do not know how that evolved, for I cannot separate the inherent from the environmental. But it seems to work for me, and that's the bottom line. I believe, and although a long-shot, the bet is for free, so I have everything to gain and nothing to lose, except my soul! Can I have faith without doubt? Is there an ocean without fish? Well, I can always swim in it, but for how long? Better get a boat, brother!

CHART OF RELIGION COMMONALITY

X = YES

	EASTERN						
	Hinduism	Buddhism	Sikhism	Janis	Confucian	Shinto	Dao/Tao
One Supreme Power	X		X				
Poly Deities	X			X		X	X
Sub Gods or Angels	X	X	X	X		X	X
Earthly Incarnations	X					X	
Teach in Parable	X	X	X	X	X	X	X
Prophets	X	X	X	X	X		X
Spirit	X		X	X		X	X
Soul	X	X	X	X		X	X
Holy Day Celebration	X	X	X	X	X	X	X
Morals and Ethics Do unto others as...	X	X	X	X	X	X	X
Do not kill	X	X	X	X	X	X	X
Do not steal	X	X	X	X	X	X	X
Do not lie	X	X	X	X	X	X	X
Good vs Evil	X	X	X	X	X	X	X
Place of Worship	X	X	X	X	X	X	X
Architecture	X	X	X	X	X	X	X
Monasteries	X	X	X	X	X	X	
Alters	X	X	X	X		X	
Art	X	X	X	X	X	X	X
Institutional Hierarchy	X	X	X	X	X	X	
Life-cycle Ritual	X	X	X	X	X	x	X
Sacrifice	X	X	X	X		X	
Forgiveness	X	X	X	X	X	X	X
Prayer	X	X	X	X	X	X	X
Afterlife	X	X	X	X	X	X	X
Holy Scripture	X	X	X	X	X	X	X

X = YES	WESTERN				
	Judean	Christian	Islam	Baha i	Mormon
One Supreme Power	X	X	X	X	X
Poly Deities					
Sub Gods or Angels	X	X	X		X
Earthly Incarnations		X	X	X	
Teach in Parable	X	X	X	X	X
Prophets	X	X	X	X	X
Spirit	X	X	X	X	X
Soul	X	X	X	X	X
Holy Day Celebration	X	X	X	X	X
Morals and Ethics					
Do unto others as…	X	X	X	X	X
Do not kill	X	X	X	X	X
Do not steal	X	X	X	X	X
Do not lie	X	X	X	X	X
Good vs Evil	X	X	X	X	X
Place of Worship	X	X	X	X	X
Architecture	X	X	X	X	X
Monasteries	X	X			
Alters	X	X	X		X
Art	X	X	X	X	X
Institutional Hierarchy	X	X	X		X
Life-cycle Ritual	X	X	X	X	X
Sacrifice	X	X	X		X
Forgiveness	X	X	X	X	X
Prayer	X	X	X	X	X
Afterlife	X	X	X	X	X
Holy Scripture	X	X	X	X	X

X = YES	NATIVE				
	Am Indian	Inca	Aztec	Aboriginal	African
One Supreme Power	X		X		X
Poly Deities	X	X	X	X	X
Sub Gods or Angels	X				X
Earthly Incarnations	X	X		X	X
Teach in Parable	X	X	X	X	X
Prophets					
Spirit	X	X	X	X	X
Soul	X	X	X		X
Holy Day Celebration	X	X	X	X	X
Morals and Ethics					
Do unto others as...	X	X	X	X	X
Do not kill	X	X	X		
Do not steal	X	X	X	X	
Do not lie	X	X	X		
Good vs Evil	X	X	X	X	X
Place of Worship	X	X	X	X	X
Architecture		X	X	X	
Monasteries					
Alters		X	X	X	X
Art	X	X	X	X	X
Institutional Hierarchy					
Life-cycle Ritual	X	X	X	X	X
Sacrifice	X	X	X	X	X
Forgiveness	X	X	X	X	X
Prayer	X	X	X	X	X
Afterlife	X	X	X		X
Holy Scripture					

bullet bob, is there a dark side to religion?

Of, course!   There are many, but the need and the bright seem to outnumber the dark.   Because it is institutionalized , power is created. Where there is power, there is corruption. Politics, politics and more politics! Combine power and passion and some bad things evolve even by the righteous. War, crusade, invasion, destruction, inquisitions, divisive preaching and power seeking to name a few.   Such a paradox, like a necessary evil. **Can you think of anything created by man without flaw**? Do you believe our great spiritual heroes like Jesus, Mohamed, Buddha, et al had an inkling of the possibility of corruption in the institutions that were created by their teachings?

bullet bob,   what is the bright side to religion?

Wow, there are numerous bright sides!   First of all, religion gives us life support with messages of hope, forgiveness, compassion and salvation. Religion is the foundation of society law and order. Religions are huge contributors in the development and maintenance of our moral and ethical system. The moral and ethical teachings of religion have huge impact on secular law Religion is a charitable institution that provides welfare in the form of shelter, money, food, clothing, job search and all basic needs of living. Religion sponsors and organizes all sorts of social programs including club meetings, competitive sports, youth camps, fund raising, and just about all basic community activities.   Religion is and has been the inspiration for the creation of wondrous architecture, namely, Pyramids, Cathedrals, Mosques, Temples, also world-class portrait and sculpture art.   Religions are extremely active in education from pre-school to major universities where huge contributions to physical science, mathematics, astronomy and medicine originate.   Lastly to mention, although there is much more, is the creation of sacred literature like the Bible, Qur'an, Vedas, Upanishads, Analects, Dhammapada, Talmud. Kohiki and Bayan.

bullet bob, is there a best religion?

Maybe? Is there a best automobile to take you to a destination? It is a matter of choice because religions take you to the similar destinations but use different vehicle and paths. Do the research; however, family, friends, and where you reside have greatest impact on your decision. I must prepare a detail discussion about the overwhelming commonality of religions and the real meaning of religious freedom.

bullet bob,   should one use the religious institution for business purposes?

Very interesting!   Do you really believe stuff like that is going on?   Need I answer this!

bullet bob,   do governments use Religion to implement policy?

Of course, all the time. **It is difficult to separate government and religion because they share common morals and ethics,** but mostly because religious institutions are very powerful. Here in the USA, where we have by constitution a separation of religion and state, the Christian Religious Right had huge voting influence in the election of Republican George W. Bush, who was advertised as a born-again Christian and when asked if he asks guidance from his father, ex-president George H. Bush, he replied that he goes to a father of higher authority for guidance. Did he use the Christian Religious Right? I think so! Was President George W a man or highest moral and ethical character? He and his administration took the USA into an unnecessary war in the middle-east and presented falsehood as reason for invasion to the entire world. Ten years of war at the cost of 6,000 US military killed, some 40,000 wounded, thousands of USA families separated, maybe 100,000 middle-easterners killed, millions displaced, infrastructure destroyed, and 3 to 4 trillion dollars added to USA national debt. Well, if there is such a thing as judgment day, George and his boys will be in a whole lot of trouble. I believe George W and aides should be tried and punished by World Court and USA Court for those immoral acts and war crimes. Who knows what was the motivation? First advertised as Sadam Hussein's weapons of mass destruction intended use and terrorist sponsorship. Both untrue! Next, protection from bin Laden the leader of al Qaeda terrorist organization, but no serious attempt to take him out. Lastly, to install democracy in Iraq and Afghanistan, which may or may not ever happen I suppose we have a moral obligation to fix what the USA destroyed in that heinous endeavor. Religion is powerful in many ways!!

bullet bob,   do religions use government to implement policy?

Yes, yes!   All the time. There are all kinds of religion/ government relationships. Works both ways!   Then there is Theocracy, where religion and government are one.

bullet bob,   if religions have so much in common, why the conflict?

Although religions have similar teachings and goals in common, they are yet very different in prophets, interpretation, structure, ritual, architecture, art, and life-style.   Kind of like automobiles, which have common purpose and function, but are different in performance and appearance. **With religion, as we do with automobiles, we focus and compete on the differences, and often lose sight of common purpose**. The ego's selfish appetite, ignorance and competitive nature of man always prevail. Is that going to change? Probably not! bullet bob changed, and sometimes he feels like a lonely dog!!

bullet bob,   Is religion a mythology?   Is government a mythology?

Yes!   Yes!   Both are huge components of the mythology of all society.

bullet bob,   What mythology do you live?

Good question.   We live in an rapidly changing world society of conflict. All the components of world mythology which include religion, government, societal norms and science are in serious conflict and have been throughout world history.   The rate of change and complexity is increasing at a rate which keeps most human beings deeply confused and mentally overloaded with voluminous conflicting social and technical information. I am also confused and have come to a decision point to choose either ignorance, a psychiatrist, or higher level of understanding. My choice is writing **"bullet bob world"**, and that is the fundamental pillar of the mythology that bullet bob lives. I believe the mythology we now live by is a rapidly changing combination of ignorance, psychiatry and misunderstanding. The modern world, you might say, has kind of lost its way in strife of a materialistic driven mythology.

bullet bob,   Do you believe the Bible stories are factual?

Well, yes and no!   However, factual or not factual really does not matter, for the message is what is really important. The message of hope, compassion, morals. ethics and eternal spirit is the foundation of all the great religions, and the use of parable or stories is the vehicle for the message. Fairy Tales, Superman and Hopalong Cassidy are great vehicles of moral/ethics messages, and do not forget the Boy and Girl Scout Oath and Creed.   All that good stuff is the foundation of the mythology that bullet bob prescribes to live by. Every day Bible stories are questioned by archeological discoveries and new scientific facts, and consequently we are in cultural transformation that confuses those who participate in a slowly dissipating Christian faith. I believe most parable of all religions was created as and should be understood as poetry. Kind of like today's commercial advertisement. We now struggle to define right and wrong, and perhaps we now prefer the absence of right and wrong. I surmise that argument is king, and long live the king of voluminous discourse and unnecessary complicated secular jargon. No wonder the proliferation of mental and physical disease. Should we strive to be more wise, compassionate, flexible progressive and open minded? Yes, yes we can do that without violating the wonderful messages of religious parable! The righteous messages delivered by fantasy stories works, and I love those stories because they are simply **fantastic**!

CRITIQUE DEMANDS PROPOSED SOLUTIONS   In this document bullet bob has been critical of government and religion for not doing a good job of informing the public. Each propagandize or preach without divulging total information and reveal only what information serves their best interest. That is not ethical and it is divisive. Each is very protective of their power. Likewise, the general public, very busy with job, toys and pleasure do not take proper time to get properly informed about government and religion matters. Consequently, this process eventually leads to some real bad actions like revolution and war. Power and greed abuse followed by violence repeats and repeats throughout history. How can the world stop this process? Probably cannot, but we must try to control this civilized madness. So, bullet bob has some suggested reform and remedy for government, religion and their constituents.

SUGGESTED REFORM FOR RELIGION   The most important remedy is to put an end to extreme doctrine and radicalization. Do not even suggest that your belief system is the best or only means to peace, forgiveness and salvation. Strongly condemn any act of violence, for there is no justification for terrorism, war or violent demonstration. Preach commonality and strive for unity of all major world religion, for your goal of peaceful worship and respect for mankind are no different than other world religion.   Stop the aggressive evangelistic activity, but welcome anyone who wishes to learn about your rich history and ritual. Avoid participation and preaching politics. Focus on peace, prayer and ritual. If your country is a theocracy or the religion has authority for government, govern with highest of moral and ethical character and support the concept of world religion unity and respect. Support and participate in the council of world religions.   Can you do those reforms?

SUGGESTED REFORM FOR GOVERNMENT   The most important remedy is to end the superiority attitude.   Conduct worldly business with total respect. Don't ever suggest that your form of government is the best for all countries. Yes, do not impose your governmental system verbally or by force. Strongly condemn all acts of violence and terrorism within and outside your country. Participate and strongly support a more powerful United Nations Organization (UN), and do not do world police activity or reaction to violence without their support (must reform the UN which include dissolution or revision of the Security Council function). Stop the sale of arms to other nations without approval of the UN. Do a better job of educating the public on how government operates and provide detail instruction of public responsibility on how to stay informed on regional and federal issues. Promote timely, total, accurate and honest information to the people. Put an end to all lobbyist activity. Where possible, keep religion separated form governmental politics (tuff job). Give equal time and attention to all nations with utmost effort to foster a friendly environment for communication and negotiation. Support the World Bank and IMF who make possible the sharing of wealth and new technology worldwide.

Specifically for the USA, I don't know where to begin, but for starters we need term limits for House of Representatives and the Senate; two terms. Lobbyist activity must be abolished by making it a criminal act on both parties. There is estimated to be 15,000 registered lobbyist in our nations' capital. Campaign donations must be limited to $100 and that is direct and indirect contributions. Make it a crime to lie and mislead in campaign advertisement on media; wow that will be a tuff assignment. Promote jobs by infrastructure investment, trade protectionism, lower tax for small business, and tax breaks for manufacturing goods in the USA. Close the tax loopholes for big business special interest. Break up the banks starting with separate commercial and investment banks. Make a law that no retirement saving funds can be invested in any form of derivative investment (options, default swaps, currency swaps, etc.). Default Swaps were major contributor to 2008 liquidity meltdown. They were sold as mortgage insurance by investment banks, insurance companies, etc. often without reserves in event of default. There was default, big time. No one knows how many default swaps existed, but some estimate the notional value more than total world net worth. No accounting requirement for these casino bets. Retirees do not want their retirement funds put at this type of risk! Only producers and business consumers of commodities allowed to participate in commodity futures trading. Reform the college loan assistance only for critical skills like Engineers and medical. Expand the existing public school system to undergraduate college, by using existing school facilities with classes day and night. Establish a single-payer government healthcare system similar to Medicare for all US citizens, for we must eliminate the financial greed by establishing a reasonable schedule of medical costs and investing in more doctors, medical equipment and medical assistants. USA has half the doctors per person when compared to many western-world countries. Today, Doctor visitors often spend more time filling out paperwork than time spent with the doctor. Medical costs can be lowered and controlled as the government can dictate a reasonable schedule of physician fees. Abolish public ownership of assault firearms and stockpiled ammunition. Establish a new immigration law whereby legal and illegal foreign workers, who have a legitimate job and abide by the law, can apply for work permits and a path for USA citizenship. They are an integral part of the USA economy, for their labor creates wealth by constructing infrastructure, picking the crops, etc. Yes the tuff jobs that most Americans prefer not to do. This is only a beginning of suggested reforms, and the existing legislature is not about to act on any of these because of their selfish behavior. The people have the power of vote, and only they can get those rascals out of Washington and replace them. Washington is broken and corrupt, and only the people can fix it. Guess I better address that right now!

SUGGESTED REFORM FOR THE PEOPLE OF USA   Over the past 30 or so years you have chosen the **easy path**. That is, the emphasis on pleasure and materialism. You have gotten fat, lazy and complacent as you enjoy the benefits of third-world labor and sacrifice. Big business has amassed unbelievable sums of money in the growing global economy by exploiting the cheap labor. The USA is now, more than ever, in a global economy, and we must learn how to adjust to this new global economy. I must be fair in saying that this global economy event has improved the quality of life worldwide, but not without a huge amount of greed by big business.

Big USA corporations gain huge profits while USA loses to many jobs. Money is power, and with that enormous money power, big corporations here in the USA have purchased favorable law making by our legislature. A sufficient number of Congressmen and Senators, hopefully not all of them, seem to have lost their righteous way and succumb to big business money in exchange for favorable legislation and regulation. A lot of that dirty money is used for election campaign needed to keep their office. **Our democracy is slipping into a moneyocracy**. I do not believe that was the intent of our constitution. Congress has had a habit of lobbying for projects that send the pork or bring home the bacon to get your vote, and in turn, sell it! Many of these projects are wasteful and add to the national debt. Is that ethical? It is downright immoral. Is that the government that you believe and give your trust? Well, the time is NOW to take time out from pleasure and choose the **hard path** which is to wise up to the fact that we have an adolescent poorly informed society that has abused the right to vote by not voting or voting in ignorance. I know it is a tuff job because of a twisted money-oriented media and twisted self-serving politicians. **Our legislature is a reflection of our society**. We have created an adolescent legislature, that act and campaign on the lowest level of moral and ethical standards. NOW is the time to take back your government and your country by voting these adolescents out of there. You do have the power, so take the hard road, do the research, use your intellect, get informed, get active, tell your friends and neighbors about this corruption. WE may be complacent, but we are not stupid! Our country is loaded with hard-working, honest, law abiding and generous people. We as a society are much better than what is going on in our government today. We have a responsibility to hold ourselves and our government to much higher standards of morality and maturity.

I know that we listen to the media broadcasters and analysts, our senators and congressmen that appear and sound so intelligent and caring, but too often they are a wolf in sheep's clothing. For the most part, their speech is money and power driven. Divisiveness speech is common. Democrats vs. Republicans. Give me a break, and save that kind of competitive mindset for the NFL and other sport events Look at the legislative gridlock caused by party-line voting in addressing almost all of important legislation and its implementation. Look at the extreme right-wing whacko Tea Party candidates elected recently. Look at the out-of-control national debt. If interest rates raise, how is the US government going to pay up? How can the US government going to pay an estimated 60 trillion in the next 10 years for committed social programs set into law? Defense, transportation. education, space exploration, et al must be paid for by Uncle Sam. There is a budget blivit. Federal government may collect 35 or 40 trillion in this next 10 years. The bottom line is **THESE GUYS ARE NOT DOING THE JOB. THEY ARE PLAYING POLITICS**. Wake up America. Shed the adolescent, for it is OK to upgrade your level of consciousness to adult maturity. It is not too late. Somehow we must replace these guys in Washington with hard working unselfish people of outstanding morals and ethics that are dedicated to a legislature that provides a robust and healthy, just and moral, proud and strong, compassionate and fair America where we protect and share in the American dream equally. We need a legislature that has a priority system whereby American people are first priority, then the party and self are second priorities in performing the duties of their elected office.

There is lot of good going on in this country which primarily is an inertial effect of good legislation and hard work of past generations, but it's eroding America, if you want to be Number One, you must think and act like Number One. Your past reputation can carry you only so far. Wake up, you are slipping. You are Number One in arms production, guns per person, drug usage, people in prison and economic consumption. You are slipping in healthcare, infrastructure, morals, ethics, recurring value production, world image, obesity, etc. America, it is time for a tune up!

Is it possible to make the following happen! **Create and present**, to all future Congressional and Senatorial candidates, **a list of reforms** that we as voters desire, and with **their signature they pledge** to introduce that legislation and support it with a yea vote. Also, a statement that they will, if elected, focus on the voices of their constituents and behold the people's welfare as sole priority in all actions while they perform the duties of their office. **If they refuse to sign, we don't vote for them**. **Very simple**. I suggest that these reforms will include:

- Amend the constitution with term limit of two for Congressmen and Senators
- A criminal offense for lobbyist activity with punishment to lobbyist, government official and staff
- A criminal offense to receive donations of more than $100 for campaign or any other office/personal activity from any one source by direct or indirect means. That includes donations from the Party system. That act will be considered legislative bribery with a two-year minimum jail sentence. Fed and local government arrange the popular TV debates.
- A simplified income tax law that uses the IRS 1959 Tax Code as a straw man with the intent to eliminate outdated, unnecessary, special interest tax lowering for all corporations especially powerful large-cap. Corporate tax rate of 20% with a special rate of 10% for business of 25 or less employees. Provide a new tax bracket for personal taxable income over 2 million dollars be taxed at the rate of 75%. Dividend income taxed as ordinary income. Capital gains at 20% tax rate up to 2 million dollars with a 75% tax rate thereafter. Inheritance taxed at 50% with 2 million dollar deduction. It is unfair, immoral and unethical to rob the company and shareholders taking outrageous salaries and stock options with outrageous low tax consequences. Generally, our tax law should support the proposition that people should be financially rewarded for efforts that produce long-term-recurring value such as labor to construct roadways and buildings, farmers, educators, medical professionals, engineers and scientists. Business managers, investors, lawyers, bean counters, food servers and professional athletes are essential to the economy, but arguably most of their effort is of non-recurring value. Investing in capitalization of others labor, personal injury suits, financial accounting, and playing sports often receive compensation way beyond their real economic value. The above income tax proposal does support this recurring vs. nonrecurring effort compensation system
- A comprehensive review of all trade policy and agreements with the intent to revise and renegotiate where practical in favor of job creation and protection here in the USA. Establish a priority of occupations that USA wishes to retain. This is a very tuff assignment because it is difficult to compete with foreign labor cost of under a US dollar. There are more than two billion foreign workers worldwide available to work at that cost, and US companies, small or huge, will find a way to exploit foreign labor. Trade deficits will remain high for a long time. USA is the king consumer; often no room for car in garage which is filled with you name it! May I say that we Americans benefit from foreign labor because the cost of goods and services here is substantially less, and worldwide especially the emerging countries have also benefited by huge increases in standards of living. American pay increases have not significantly improved, but their buying power has improved dramatically during this

globalization process. Be careful to impose higher import taxes, for it may cause serious global economic and political problems. However, I do believe it is better to retain jobs here in the USA for skill retention and mental health reasons, in spite of a very possible increase in living expenses. The loss of jobs caused by globalization and the 2008 meltdown has created a huge underground labor force, and in my opinion is great for America. Maybe they do not pay federal or state income tax, but they have gained their independence and self worth. Should underground labor and illegal drug business be included in the GNP? Sitting in meetings, counting beans, staring at computers and playing politics is counterproductive to health. Creating tangible reoccurring value like infrastructure, machinery and crops makes it easier to sleep at night and gives an awesome feeling of accomplishment and self worth .

- A complete study and review of USA major and essential infrastructure with schedule and cost that has little or no increase on national debt. Utilize government and private company partnership for investment and profit sharing in new infrastructure. The USA government is seriously in debit and needs the financial help from the private sector who have benefited from the financial generosity of the USA government. Now it is time to pay back as a partner in infrastructure renovation, after all, it is to your benefit.

- Institute a government healthcare system similar to Medicare for all Americans. The current system lacks competition due to insufficient number of doctors and insurance company/drug company profit rigging. Plan and establish the US Health Army responsible for total public healthcare which includes training of all categories of healthcare personal, operation of hospitals and clinics. Create a Health Care Army Academy. Join the Healthcare Army and get healthcare training with a 10-year service commitment The health army should take 5 years to convert today's expensive healthcare to an affordable US Health Army operation . A $10 co-pay for doctor office visits and a maximum co-pay of $600 for hospital stay should be required. The VA should be the responsibility of the new Health Army. USA has 2.5 physicians per 1,000 population with people living longer and population on the increase. So, why not avoid a crisis by immediately investing in the education of physicians, assistants and technicians. Immediately, lower the current Medicare/Medicaid medical payment schedule to a reasonable amount with a target of 1/3 cost reduction.   Start today to negotiate a reasonable cost of prescription drugs with the greedy drug companies. Employers will certainly benefit financially from this new government healthcare reform. As an alternate they can choose private insurance plans, for private practice doctors and healthcare facilities will co-exist. Why not allow purchase of most common drugs without prescription, and allow foreign drug manufactures to compete here in the USA? This new healthcare system will reduce the outrageous cost of healthcare which is now 17% of USA GNP. Most modern countries spend 8% to 12% of GNP on health care, and outrank the USA in rating by world health organizations. World-wide the USA is ranked number thirty or higher. Now we spend at least as twice per person, over $8,000, and our longevity is one or two years less than many other countries. Again, we do not eliminate private healthcare thus providing a choice. Yes, doctors, hospitals, insurance companies will take a haircut, for too long their greed has existed. USA can no longer afford their unmerciful greed perhaps caused by the cost/limiting of doctor education and mal practice insurance. The latter is lawyer greed and ridiculous cash judgments by our judicial system. Cap the cash awards and limit legal fees to 10% of cash awards and settlements. This healthcare plan may seem impossible probably because it is just and practical, for today's politicians generally don't think or act in an efficient, ethical or practical manner. Money for political power is their priority. Health is wealth! What good is money and material without good health? Just think, this unethical lame-brain bunch of politicians are responsible for the death and ill health of thousands and just may be killing themselves! Many claim to be of Christian faith and values.

- Abolish the current college loan program, but institute a 1% interest rare for student loan repayment for all existing college loans. Expand the current local public school system to undergraduate degrees. Use all existing public school system facilities with day and night classes. Do not increase federal funds to supplement the current local government school taxes to fund the expanded education system, and no financial assistance to private education institutions except for critical skill education and research. Quit throwing money to solve problems. Use imagination and innovation. Again, this enhanced public school system will lower the overall cost of education and provide greater education opportunity to all, thus a more skillful and knowledgeable national workforce. The current college loan program has allowed greedy higher educational institutions to increase tuition rates far above economic value and affordability. The quality of higher education is questionable! Stop the blame of inferior schools and teachers. Learning tools and facilities are in all schools. Parents live up to your responsibility to be good role models for education and demand good study habits and respect for the teachers and school educational facilities. Hopefully, we can put families back together again. School administrators please live up to your responsibility to provide facilities and curriculums that provide outstanding skill in the three R's and focus on the natural abilities and passion of the students. As skill needs change, our schools at all levels must provide facilities and programs to train and retrain workers to satisfy national skill requirements. I know it is a tuff job to match skill requirements with natural ability and passion, but I am sure it can be done if the teaching profession puts their God-given mind to task. Get the politicians out of public school systems, and leave managing to professional educators. Reduce the size of the Department of Education by at least 50% and limit responsibility to education formula funding to states, critical skill education funding, critical research funds to universities and national testing standards.
- A criminal offense for private ownership of automatic and semiautomatic firearms, explosive materials and excessive ammunition. Require criminal and sanity background check and registration for all gun purchases. Only federal government authorized dealers can buy, sell or exchange guns for public use. No gun or ammunition exchanges at trade shows, internet or private exchange. With about 300 million firearms now here in the USA, this is a huge and almost impossible problem in combating gun violence.
- Legislation to provide work permits and a path for USA citizenship for honest, hard working illegal workers. Secure the south border. Provide work permits for essential labor and enforce current deportation law. The USA economy is heavily dependent on foreign labor. Retain the contributors and deport the undesirable. Immigration policy must focus on national security and national skill requirements like medical doctors and scientists of all kinds. Hopefully, some of the foreign higher-education students will stay here after graduation
- Reform the criminal justice system with maximum of 10 years in prison for non-violent crimes. Incorrigible repeat offenders, death sentence and life sentence offenders be exiled (a new Devils Island ?) . It is inhumane and extremely expensive to incarcerate 2.2 million prisoners here in the USA. Maximize behavior reform training and minimize punishment for non-violent and domestic crimes.
- Reform the Defense Department, the Pentagon, for it takes much too long to development

new war equipment and at a ridiculous cost. Reduce the size of the pentagon staff by at least 50 percent and give the contractors more decision responsibility as we did in WW II and the cold war. Stop the steady transition of pentagon armed forces retirees to military equipment contractors by making it illegal, for it appears there is collusion in negotiating extremely ridiculous high cost of war goods.

- Increase the Social Security retirement eligibility age to 70 with no early retirement provision. Cap the wage takeout rate for employees and employer at today's rate with an $80,000 ceiling.   Healthcare and Pentagon reform will pay for this reduced takeout rate.

- Government deficit spending must be abolished by eliminating inefficient wasteful spending. We must not only balance the budget but create surplus, or we face economic disaster. We must replace trying to solve all problems with throwing money at it, with common sense innovation. Nothing is off-the-table in budget reduction. Yes, this is a do or die exercise. Everybody must participate in sacrifice, and the budget should reflect a fair and just participation. We cannot spend trillions on unnecessary wars and world police activity without country and personal economic sacrifice. We must put greed, foolish pride and politics aside!! It can be done, for it only takes will power, common sense and smart sacrifices. I can only compare the kind of sacrifice very possible to two events in the past 100 years, and that is depression and WW II. Let's not let that happen!

- Reduce substantially the number of military in foreign countries especially in Japan, South Korea and Germany where approximately 40,000 USA military reside in each of those countries. After 50 to 70 years of military support and protection, it's about time for them to step up their military. USA can no longer provide world-wide police activity at current level, for not only economically costly it is foolish. USA can lead this police endeavor , but we need substantially more help from our friends and allies. Strive to strengthen the role of the United Nations Organization. Please rethink and renegotiate the current world-wide military deployment with a 50% reduction by year 2020.

- Stop the emphasis on abortion legislation. Leave that business to the individual and their maker.   Support planned parenthood and responsible sex education.

- Stop the emphasis on same-sex marriage debate. Abolish the term "marriage" in legal documentation and use the term "union".

- Note: The above two issues probably will not destroy our country, but a failing legislature, runaway national debt and unnecessary war promotion for sure will destroy our country.

Many of this list of suggested reform may appear somewhat extreme and communistic. I believe that our form of government is a combination of free-market capitalism and common-sense communism. Both are essential and must be in balance. Capitalism has a greed problem, and communism has a greed problem. Both must be bound by morals, ethics and common sense legislation. Unfortunately, man is flawed with greed, and it seems that there are no limits to greed. Thus, we create more and more laws and regulations by our government, which gets bigger and bigger. Well, maybe Marx and Engels were correct about the evolution of government growth and control. Our predecessors, Europeans, often have the appearance of greater governmental control and some refer to that as extreme and communistic. Since the American spirit is very much risk taker, hard work ethic and learns from mistakes, there is little chance of becoming a predominately communistic-oriented government. Our open and free business market economy will prevail. Universal healthcare and free public education along with high taxation for income that does not provide recurring value, does not make USA communistic. That just makes the USA more moral, ethical and common sense oriented. Everything changes including our government. Right now our legislature is hampered by influx of special interest money to rig elections and legislative agenda. Reform is necessary. Reform will happen! Do you know that our original Constitution has almost doubled in page count because of amendments!

Why is the little or no discussion about term limits and although discussed, no reform action on lobbyist activity or monetary donations to candidates and government officials? Fat chance that lawmakers will pass legislation that possibly eliminates their job and party status. How loyal to country and greedy is that! Looks like money rules, and who is really governing the country? Our legislature is trusted to carry out their job to the highest moral and ethical standards. They should be immune to financial and special interest greed. They work for all the people with no special law treatment to rich people, corporations and other organizations able to buy their election and subsequent lawmaking activities. The very foundation of our government is corrupted by career politicians sponsored by special interest financing. This is wrong, so let's reform and eliminate this corrupt government greed system. Right now we Americans have a damn good life, but this corrupted political system sooner or later will lead to our downfall financially and morally. The American dream may become a nightmare.

Somehow, America has to simplify the legal documentation. The volume and complication is ridiculous, for who has time to read, interpret and maintain this massive jargon of high fog index. The lawyers have created a self-fulfilling job of analysis and argument. I know the world is complicated, but I believe law should be written for an eighth-grade graduate to understand without doubt or question. What a waste of physical and mental energy that can be applied to essential quality of life matters. **Simplicity is the essence of design**. Not only impossible but impractical to attempt to satisfy every American and all special interest groups. What happened to self-reliance and common sense?

Well, if we the people can somehow find and elect candidates that meet and institute these reforms, it would be a miracle, but as bullet bob says "if it is thinkable, it is possible". Actually, if we want to get this country to stop the decline and be the country of high standards that we individually and collectively aspire, we must get politically smart and peacefully revolt using the power of vote to reform to a more efficient and ethical government. Right now our country is becoming exactly what our enemies criticize. It will be a long and rigorous task, but it is inevitable that reform for the best will happen sooner or later. Well, that's the American way throughout history. Namely, we respond to crisis. The sleeping giant wakes up and becomes a hero. America gets fixed, then goes to sleep again, totally unaware of a future crisis. So be it. Never count America out. Only a fool would bet against America. bullet bob says that NOW is time for the sleeping giant to wake up. Please, America Public, WAKE UP!

Meanwhile, bullet bob is making plans to visit Thailand, a country using the American economic model in quest of economic growth and standard of living improvement. They do have governmental corruption problems, but the recent street demonstration by tens of thousands has resulted in the ouster of the corrupt and the transition to a new peoples' government. This transition is directed by the military with blessing of the King and will take perhaps two years or more to write a new constitution and purge the government agencies of corruption before a new elected government is installed. Meanwhile there is genuine peace and thriving business economy. Bangkok now ranks as one of the largest retail centers in the world. It is modernizing at a fast pace with modern rail, natural gas street vehicles, and probably the world's most modern and efficient international airport, which hosts about 65 million travelers each year. They have universal healthcare for all Thai citizens with prompt and state-of-the-art medical staff and facilities, no sales tax, and most individuals pay little or no income tax. There is a huge underground economy of farmers, street vendors and laborers. There are modern private hospitals, very efficient and very reasonably affordable for visitors and provide an alternate.

 From my observations over the past six years in Southeast Asia, I would say that the future major world development is in Asia Of course, labor is under a dollar (US). American labor is at huge competitive disadvantage. USA is a leader in technology, but seems we give away that technology (intellectual property) in the process of using the cheap labor of the emerging world to manufacture the goods. Yes, we have a double whammy loss of jobs and intellectual property advantages. Money rules! The future is now in the global economy, and adjusting to it here in the USA is a major challenge.

 I have addressed just a few of USA internal challenges and have not addressed external challenges with exception of cursory world-trade reform discussion. The world is changing at a fast pace with violent revolution in middle-east, world-wide terrorist activity growing, world-wide potential war threats, climate change, starvation and energy conservation to name a few. The world is changing at a very fast pace, so we need a government in the USA that is alert, astute, ethical, and quick to act if USA is to keep up with a fast pace world. Ideally, stay ahead of the world and internal game. Our legislature and political system is now broken and is not keeping up. We participate in our political party system like professional sports teams, and by far the most important thing is winning regardless of lies, rule violations, unfairness and finding new ways to cheat. We, as a country, are falling behind. We may go broke. Go visit the emerging countries of the world and observe new and modern infrastructure, latest technology and standard-of-living improvement. You, the voting public, have ultimate responsibility for the direction of this country. Live up to your responsibility, get informed, define the quality of candidates, find them, vote them in and get the current bunch of rotten apples in legislature out of there. We can no longer afford this system of unethical, selfish, adolescent, unqualified, slow moving, uncompromising, party-oriented stooges guiding this country. These guys are incompetent in serving the people. Not bad in serving themselves. Remember that your legislature is a reflection of the people that elected them. Yes, you can take the effort to improve your understanding of government and it's challenges. I am confident you will make right choices in voting a much better legislature that focuses on **right-for-country** legislation. It is a must!

I must point out that given to the most angelic angel the gift of power that angel will eventually become corrupt. I believe our constitution is guided by that principle. Term limits of Congressmen and Senators is now essential since it seems the angel-corruption transformation process occurs in a very short time. Especially, this applies to career politicians and lawyers. Beware of horse traders and car dealers, but now politicians and lawyers go at the top of the list of the least trusted.

bullet bob,   does the Western World have a violence problem?

Here in the USA there seems to be an addiction to violence. Yes, we can't get enough of it!
Violence dominates TV news, TV prime-time entertainment, movies, computer games, pop-rock
music, UFC, and hugely successful American football.   Violence begets violence! The
glorification of violence created by the media can and does have a negative impact on the mind
and likewise society behavior. I can't think of a better way to become popular than to commit
some form of violence. News broadcasters thrive on violence and use it for making money.
Look at the many protest movements that get an unbelievable amount of media time and
attention. Look at the large number of westerners leaving their country to join terrorist ISIS or
commit savage terrorist actions in their residing country. Look at the mentally-disturbed and
anti-government nut cases in the USA that murder innocent victims at public institutional
gatherings. Look at the gang killings almost like routine.

Combine the corrupt government legislature, glorified violence, money-minded media and
expanding drug culture, our country becomes fertile territory for radicalization and recruitment.
Our enemies could not be happier other than engaging the USA and the western world in all out
war with subsequent occupation activity which is unaffordable! The huge USA and western-
world countries national debt and deficit spending yields a very precarious economies. Our
enemies know that and taunt us into economic stress.

bullet bob,   what can be done about this negative behavior?

This is a very complex group of problems and maybe unsolvable to eliminate, but I believe a
drastic reduction in this negative behavior can be achieved by doing the following:

- Responsible media coverage like minimum reporting on violent acts
- Immediate and quick justice for murderous and terrorist crimes
- Elect honest, mature, common-sense, country-first local and federal legislature
- Stop the emphasis on violence presented in movies, TV and hard-rock pop music

Generally, USA society should shed the ignorance and shift focus from violence to tranquility,
from materialism to common sense, and it is OK to improve your consciousness from adolescent
to maturity.

bullet bob,   will USA fix these problems, and who will lead the fix?

Can all the king's horses, and all the king's men
put humpty dumpy back together again?

bullet bob,   how should USA deal with ISIS, ISIL, and other terrorist organizations?

The Obama administration is trying to minimize USA life and money expenditures by supporting anti-ISIS fighters with training, munitions and air bombing. Let the middle easterners and Africans fight their war battles. Often not easy to determine who to support due to the many religious factions, tribes, countries and civil war groups involved, all with mixed war agendas. USA trained and supported Iraqi and Syrian fighters often do not fight very well, but eventually they must step up. So, this strategy isn't working as well as desired, but will improve. The terrorist threat is now worldwide especially the western world and is disruptive and costly money wise as well as restrict freedom. Our police, intelligence and anti-terrorist organizations worldwide are doing a good job of coordinating efforts to protect us at home and abroad. No real serious attempt to form a world-wide military coalition to defeat these savages in their homelands. ISIS et al, have an abundance of money, arms suppliers and oil which has not been dismantled by current war efforts. Now there is stalemate. Perhaps, a coalition will be formed with USA leading a long, difficult, expensive campaign including many years of occupation effort all of which we cannot afford. USA needs troop and financial contribution from allies of which they cannot afford. Should we bring back Harry Truman?

May I point out that this war in the middle-east and parts of Africa along with world-wide terrorist activity is spiritually driven. This world-wide terrorist activity may be enhanced by western world political unrest. We are fighting a spirit which may never be eliminated but only controlled. After all, the people of these countries have been physically and economically repressed by dictatorships for many many generations, extremely angry and hungry for power. The coalition may defeat ISIS/ ISIL, et al or get them under control, but until the formation of stable governments that provide economies of jobs and modern standards-of-living, there will be a high level of violence like car bombing, mass shooting, bomb planting and other violent terrorist acts. This process will take generations to get it under acceptable control. This will be a tuff job for the United States and the rest of the world countries to figure out how to deal with this spiritually-driven terrorist-minded war and the subsequent stabilization. The physical part of land control can be achieved in a fairly short time, say a year or two, after an international anti-terrorism collation is formed and acts. That is, take back control of the land and economic assets. However, the psychological part of defeating a spirit will require improving minds using population cleansing, educational and economic strategy as well as installation of trusted stable governments. We must keep in mind that these terrorist groups do not wear uniforms as in traditional war, and when they lose the land battle, simply unite with the general population and go underground or to a remote desolate location. The most extensive search and capture missions may control violence but never extinguish. The USA and allies are not ready to accept the loss, injury and displacement of human lives as well as the financial cost to do this job. The middle easterners and Africans must step up to do the ground fighting, violence control, infrastructure rebuilding and establishment of trusted governments. An international coalition must assume a support role, but hard to define that support role due to the lack of homeland support and all having substantial government indebtedness. Right now, I see no political will to build an urgent international strategy to get this inevitable difficult task executed. The western world now may have too many domestic economic and political problems to deal with. I doubt if the United Nations has the power and influence to get this job done. Well, this intolerable is currently tolerable! Is it hopeless? What about a political solution via negotiation with terrorist groups? Thinkable but maybe not possible because it is not practical nor reasonable to negotiate with this deep-seeded, radicalized, evil spirit. I believe cancer will be eliminated before this problem is solved.

Meanwhile, the President and all elected government officials have got to inform all of us that the terrorist threat has no boundaries, and everybody has a duty to participate by being vigilant to possible homeland terrorist threats. Please keep in mind that there will be forever government and society dissenters, and the current terrorist threat adds imputes for dissenter individuals to act out their violent thoughts. Now, combine the readily available guns and munitions, it is simply a more dangerous world. Consequently, everyone that suspects terrorist threats or possible violent activity has a duty to report it to the police or intelligence agency for investigation. I do not recommend creation of a special agency to deal with the suspicious terrorist activity, but the federal and local government can provide and publicize a common telephone number to report suspicious terrorist activity here in USA. For example: "811". I hope the investigative activity can be done and coordinated with the current investigative agencies without massive recruitment of additional manpower. I suspect there is competition and distrust among our police and investigative agencies, but now is the time to put that aside. We must foster an international cooperative effort of world-wide police and intelligence organizations. May the spirit of WW II resurrect. We are in this (I do not like to call it war) together, like it or not, we are all now **citizen soldiers**.

MISTER bullet bob,   WOULD YOU LIKE TO BE PRESIDENT OF THE USA?

Although it is a very dangerous job, I would like to be President but only with reservation. First of all, I would accept no pay for my service. I would ride to Washington on a white horse wearing a mask, white hat and gun belt with loaded six gun in my holster. I would meet with all Congressional and Senatorial members to draft and pass all my proposed legislation ready for my signature. This will take about one workday or 8 hours. No legislative bill will require more than one page, double-space, elite type. After I sign the legislation into law, I will resign the Presidency, get on my white horse and gallop out of that despicable place. Hopefully not too many bullets will be missing when I depart. By the way, these are bullet bob bullets loaded with morals, ethics and common sense.

I can hear those petty politicians asking, "Who in the hell was that masked man"?

And some young black fellow replies,

"That was president bullet bob, the mild-mannered old dog. Suggest you don't mess with him"!

 "Where did he come from? Where's he going?"

  "Don't really know. He just goes around doing good stuff"

"How do you know of him?"

"Everybody knows him. He's kinda like **Good.** Man, just where has your heads been hang'n out?"

bullet bob,   why not use gas instead of bullets?

Well, that's a great idea!   But I am bullet bob, not gas bob! **gas bob? I want to be remembered as a hero, not a shit ass!**

Just a little more

Aggravation

Illusion

TELEPHONE ANSWERING MENUS   Often there are three levels of menu items, and often I get confused in making a selection. However, to speak to a real person also becomes a problem because the person speaks with a strange foreign accent, does not have the business knowledge and authority. You must be placed on hold, listen to some bad music while waiting for second, third and maybe a fourth specialist. Each specialist for security and identification purposes asks the same questions. The chances of a satisfactory telephone call are about 50 percent. Yes, it is not unusual to spend an hour on the phone about a three-minute business item. I hate to call any institution, government or other business, for it is so frustrating. I can't imagine the business man-hours wasted as a result of this activity. This is just one of the many abuses of automation implementation.   I believe that customer satisfaction is most important, but apparently I must be wrong.

TATOS AND PIERSING   At some time in your life you will wish to remove them. This could be a real problem.   To me, this represents poor judgment, bad taste, and immaturity. This activity can produce a lot of bad experiences, like separate you from mainstream society, close doors of opportunity, cause infection and very expensive. Those with multi or large tattoos are beyond my rationality and they are branded for life. Often the tattoos lack artistry and symbolize weird activity or events. What's going on?

MEDIA ADVERTISING   In general there is too much advertising and often it is misleading or sometimes an outright lie.   Television and radio are loaded with so many commercials that I continually switch stations or channels to avoid them. Make a law to limit TV and radio ads to 5 minutes per hour. The biggest trash item today is mail advertising. What a huge waste provided by the big money loser, the USPS.

Many commercials use fear themes while others use pornographic themes. I believe this is unethical and especially unethical to advertise prescription drugs and legal services. The first ad says take the drug, and the next ad says sue the drug company.

Any offer and especially an offer with an asterisk* is probably misleading and borders the category of lie. Ads are designed to trick you. When reading the fine print it may be voluminous and carries a high fog index.

Many TV commercials are so abstract that I get confused, and there seems to be no continuity to the product or service. Yes, attention getters! The majorities of TV commercials are poorly done and lack symbolic meaning or entertainment value.

MOST RADIO TALK SHOW HOSTS   The very worse is the extremely narrow-minded Sean Hannity. He is a nice looking guy with a great gift of gab, but so immature. Next in line is Rush Linbaugh, the EIBS(Excellence in Bullshit) network. He has a great imagination when giving his analysis of what is really going on. He takes an insignificant item and makes a huge insightful issue. He is for the most part a fraud, and I doubt if he believes most of what he broadcasts. Don't take him seriously, but enjoy the entertainment, the fantasy, the shock, and the controversy. Don't take all he says as truth. Unfortunately, I believe that some people do take him seriously

How about Michael Savage, the brilliant, resourceful, righteous scholar. Take away the violence and extreme criticism of everybody and everything and you have something special. I enjoy and agree with much he has to say, but the underlying violence and ego seem to override the brilliance of which he is capable.

Bill ORielly is a very talented communicator, but he is such a hypocrite and most often on the wrong side of history. Bill, Mr. Generous, votes his pocket book rather than best for country. The choice of heavy makeup and tight clothing on his female guests is crass and downright ugly. His stage buddy, Dennis Miller, has a mind beyond twisted and his satire is stupid, not funny. Dennis is the perfect candidate as poster boy for national contraceptive century. Watters World is stolen from Jay Leno/Johnny Carson Tonight Show and loses it humor impact with a very needless movie cameo format. How much does Bill contribute to writing all those books? With his name so big on the cover it must be a huge contribution, ha!

I can name many more hosts, but I will stop here. It seems all of them have the ability to create controversy and get attention. The real value is that they may inspire all of us to learn enough about a political topic to develop an intelligent opinion and hopefully express it.

PARENTS AT CHILDREN'S SPORT EVENTS   First of all, most parents are fat, and they need the exercise more than the children who participate. Don't they realize that a huge part of parenting is to be a good example for the children? Sad but true that the children will probably grow into fat, uninspired, under achievers just like the parents. Often the children are treated like toys and more often the children rule. The adolescent parents have not matured and seem to relive their youth via the offspring. Seems like the kids participate only when the parents attend. That is strange, and where is the passion? Where is the initiative on the part of the children? No wonder the high divorce rate, for the marriage and the family will probably not grow beyond the adolescent phase. Never to mature into an intimate blissful experience. What chance do the children and the parents can realize their potential?

DOCTOR OFFICE VISITS   The office visit begins with payment arrangements and CYA (doctor not responsible for anything) paperwork. Do we not get the impression that the money is more important than healing the patient? Then, there is the wait for the call with year-old travel magazines to entertain you. After a half-hour wait you get the call and are escorted to lonely room filled with medical supplies. The medical assistant checks vital signs. Another fifteen-minute wait until the doctor arrives. After reviewing your medical file he asks, "How are you?" You say, "Just fine except for this problem". Shortly thereafter the doctor (or medical assistant) scribbles on the prescription pad and says, "Take this medication as prescribed." You ask, "What's the diagnosis?" He or she or it uses a few medical terms which you have only a clue. The doctor conversation lasts less than five minutes. You are afraid to ask questions because you do not want to take up the doctor's precious time. There are others waiting. You leave but not fully satisfied and a bit confused. If there was a serious health problem the doctor will refer you to a specialist. Maybe you are escorted to the doctor's main office. The one with mahogany furniture and walls filled with diplomas and awards. Another fifteen-minute wait for the specialist referral. Before leaving the office, you may find out the cost of the office visit and pay the co-payment. Wow, this is expensive and what would I do if I had no insurance? You then look at the prescription and cannot read it. Hope the pharmacist can read it. Hope I get the right medication.

Upon arrival at home you go to the computer and surf the web and find a fairly detailed discussion about the prescribed medication, which includes dosage, symptoms, and side effects. Also, for what disease the medication is prescribed. Why not consult the computer instead of the doctor? Because often you need a doctor's prescription to buy the medication, but was doctor knowledge and experience really needed to make an accurate diagnosis? Was it accurate?

DRUG BLAME   Mexico or Mexican drug cartels are most to blame for USA drug problems. Really! Where there is demand, it will be satisfied. The demand is at all levels of USA society. To eliminate the demand is probably impossible, because major reform in all aspects of USA society is required. Too huge to discuss here. It would take volumes stacked to your eyebrows, and maybe that would be a waste of time. I see no viable solution, for it is major cancer of world society yesterday, today and tomorrow. So more blame, more laws, more jails, more search & seizers, more killing, more treatments. It will be interesting to see the social and political impact of recreational marijuana legalization.

bullet bob you are quite the critic. How long have you been so critical?

Ever since I was a puppy! After all, bullet bob is a true American, and that's what Americans do best!

One day I visited an art exhibition. I am not a huge fan of portrait art, but to satisfy my curiosity I wanted to discover the pleasure that artists and collectors of art experience. By the way, I classify art in three categories which are repulsive, likeable or sublime pleasure. Some call it rapture.

Most of the art at the gallery fit the repulsive category, and a few were likeable and interesting. However one painting just stopped me in my tracks and captured my total awareness and curiosity. The name of the painting was "The Virgin". I did not look to see the name of the artist who painted this most beautiful young lady of extraordinary radiance. I observed the absolute model of feminine physical perfection and innocents. As I focused on her delicate facial features, her soft blue eyes, her full lips and her blondish hair which was pinned upward with dangling curls, my consciousness was raptured. I recalled that pinned up hair is the signature of virginity.

Yes, my imagination went adrift. My consciousness now sublime. I have no idea how long I remained in sublimation, but I do remember the beautiful virgin invited me to enter the painting. I accepted the invitation. Stepped into the frame. She took my hand, and we fled to a secluded cottage where she shed her clothing and led me to the bedroom. She unbuttoned my shirt, unbuckled my belt and pulled me to the bed. To describe the consummate passionate sexual experience is beyond possibility because my pen and hand are not worthy of such extraordinary sublime pleasure.

Totally exhausted we returned to the exhibit site. I kissed her soft lips and stepped out of the painting back to the floor. The gallery attendant nudged me to inform that it was closing hour. Extremely exhausted and totally sensually satisfied, I struggled to my 1984 Chevy pickup truck that somehow carried me home and fully clothed went straight to bed.

On awaking the next day I dressed and returned to the art exhibit with full remembrance of yesterday's sublime pleasure. I hurried to the site of the painting. Why did I return? It seemed so real! I was confused. Is it possible to visit the sublime experience once more? As I approached the portrait, once again my consciousness transcended by the most beautiful lady of extraordinary radiance. Something in the painting was different. The portrait had changed. Her hair was no longer pinned. **IT WAS DOWN!**

bullet bob, that was an illusion!

Yes, maybe that is true. But what is the difference? Is it not the very same sensation? Is this world just one grand illusion? My subconscious tells me so!

bullet bob, will you return to the portrait site?

Yes. I return often. I offer to purchase the portrait and the secluded cottage, but so far, neither for sale!

PERPLEXED   I have given "bullet bob world" to about a dozen friends and family and have **not received one comment of substance.** I ask myself, **why?** Authors say do not test your writing with family and friends. I have a few guesses and now present them as follows:

The topics are of religion and politics which are politically incorrect to discuss in today's society. It is controversial subjects which could cause hard feelings and bring about strong emotions that most do not wish to deal with.

The reader strongly disagrees with bullet bob on many of his conclusions on religion and politics.   bullet bob presents his world in hope of challenge and discussion to see how others view these controversial topics **in a spirit of learning and understanding.**

The reader is not interested. After all, it is written by bullet bob who is no real authority nor the intellect to discuss such matters.

The reader is not spiritually or politically mature or just not ready to deal with such intimate subjects.   After all, we do live, that is for the vast majority, in **a society of adolescent.**

Perhaps, **bullet bob world** is loaded with discussion that requires the reader to use a lot of think energy, which is very hard. That kind of think energy is reserved for **money making and hobbies.**

Perhaps the readers look at bullet bob's presentation and find it simple blabber which they have read and thought about. Nothing new or original.

The reader, for the most part, does not agree and does not wish to waste time discussing, especially with an old dog!

SELF PSYCHOANAYSIS   bullet bob had a bit of mental breakdown. The old dog imagined himself on the heroes' journey where he departs mentally from societies' norm on a lonely hallucinated trip where only intellectual help from others is needed to cure this possible psychosis. Can he return to societies' acceptable norm? Is bullet bob, the old dog, crazy or achieved a higher level of consciousness or a little of both???

CONCLUSION   It has been fun writing **bullet bob world**. Hope someone has fun reading it. Sorry, but I am still perplexed. Hopefully, a little bit wiser, but just a little disappointed not able to connect intellectually. So be it.

Farewell, Farewell.   From the beginning there was little doubt,
The mighty wasteland wins, bullet bob gracefully, bow wows out!

THAT'S ALL FOLKS!